Whitman and the American Idiom

Whitman and the American Idiom

MARK BAUERLEIN

LOUISIANA STATE UNIVERSITY PRESS
Baton Rouge and London

DESIGNER: PATRICIA DOUGLAS CROWDER
TYPEFACE: LINOTRON 202 ALDUS
TYPESETTER: G&S TYPESETTERS, INC.
PRINTER AND BINDER: THOMSON-SHORE, INC.

LIBRARY OF CONGRESS CATALOGING-IN-PUBLICATION DATA

Bauerlein, Mark.
    Whitman and the American idiom / Mark Bauerlein.
    p.   cm.
    Includes bibliographical references and index.
    ISBN 0-8071-1681-5 (cloth : alk. paper)
    1. Whitman, Walt, 1819–1892—Criticism and interpretation.
    2. National characteristics, American, in literature.
    3. Americanisms in literature.   I. Title.
    PS3238.B34   1991
    811'.3—dc20   91-10929
                                                   CIP

The author is grateful to the editors of the following journals for permission to reprint material from his previously published articles that have appeared under these titles: "The Written Orator of 'Song of Myself': A Recent Trend in Whitman Criticism," *Walt Whitman Quarterly Review* (Winter, 1986), 1–14; "Whitman's Language of the Self," *American Imago* (Summer, 1987), 129–48.

The paper in this book meets the guidelines for permanence and durability of the Committee on Production Guidelines for Book Longevity of the Council on Library Resources. ∞

to Danielle

Contents

Acknowledgments

My thanks go to Barbara Packer and Samuel Weber for reading portions of the manuscript and offering helpful advice and insights as to its content and language. I also thank Lois Geehr for editing the manuscript and bringing its syntax and style to fruition. I owe my greatest thanks to Joseph N. Riddel, whose instruction and friendship have proved to be an abiding inspiration for me. He has been and will continue to be an exemplary model of professional integrity and critical acumen.

Abbreviations

Cor   *The Correspondence of Walt Whitman.* Edited by Edwin Haviland Miller. 6 vols. New York, 1961–77.

DN   *Daybooks and Notebooks.* Edited by William White. 3 vols.
New York, 1978.

In Re   *In Re Walt Whitman.* Edited by Horace Traubel, Richard
Maurice Bucke, and Thomas B. Harned. Philadelphia, 1893.

LG   *Leaves of Grass: A Textual Variorum of the Printed Poems.*
Edited by Sculley Bradley, Harold W. Blodgett, Arthur Golden,
and William White. 3 vols. New York, 1980.

LGCRE   *Leaves of Grass: Comprehensive Reader's Edition.* Edited by
Harold W. Blodgett and Sculley Bradley. New York, 1965.

NUPM   *Notebooks and Unpublished Prose Manuscripts.* Edited by
Edward F. Grier. 6 vols. New York, 1984.

Pr   *An American Primer.* Edited by Horace Traubel. Cambridge,
Mass., 1904.

PW   *Prose Works, 1892.* Edited by Floyd Stovall. 2 vols. New York,
1963–64.

WWC   *With Walt Whitman in Camden.* Edited by Horace Traubel *et
al.* 6 vols. Vol. I, Boston, 1906; Vol. II, New York, 1908; Vol.
III, New York, 1914; Vol. IV, Philadelphia, 1953; Vol. V, Carbondale, Ill., 1964; Vol. VI, Carbondale, Ill., 1982.

Introduction

Judging from the history of Whitman scholarship and criticism, one would not consider that Whitman was a theoretical poet and that his poetry demanded a theoretical approach. The best-known figures in the long and distinguished tradition of Whitman studies (Emory Holloway, Floyd Stovall, Gay Wilson Allen, Richard Chase, James E. Miller, Jr., Roger Asselineau, Edwin Haviland Miller, Paul Zweig, William White) have usually assumed a biographical or psychological perspective, choosing to read the poems for their historical or psychic content and passing over the problematic relation between life and literature, content and style, intention and expression, meaning and sign, and other representational oppositions that theory often takes as its subject matter.

These professional readers of *Leaves of Grass* are out to explain what the poems mean, what they refer to—not to reflect upon how they express meaning or upon what special linguistic problems of meaning or reference they raise. Although many scholars have often raised questions involving language and meaning, in traditional scholarship those questions generally appear as a conflict between a democratic poet and an aristocratic literary heritage, a sensitive poetic imagination and a repressive family background, or a visionary soul striving after the infinite and a mundane urban environment of deadening particulars. In each case (all are significant and applicable to the poetry), the former triumphs over the latter through the poet's discovery and development of a native, vernacular poetic idiom congenial to the liberated self and in accordance with New World realities. In other words, to most Whitman scholars,

1

many of whose works are models of incisive criticism and painstaking research, the American bard's founding dilemma is primarily that of finding a way to break free of a stifling literary tradition and to transcend an uninspiring social and political climate. Whether language can facilitate transcendence and whether it can achieve some pure origination are issues the critical tradition has not extensively addressed.

But the situation is virtually the opposite in criticism devoted to theoretical interpretations of American literature. In American studies, when theoretical speculation takes precedence over historical research, Whitman is often relegated to a negligible position. In works by noteworthy Americanist professors whose theories of American writing have influenced the way American Renaissance texts have been read and taught, R. W. B. Lewis, Charles Feidelson, Leslie Fiedler, Richard Poirier, Sacvan Bercovitch, and John Irwin spend merely a few pages or parts of a chapter on Whitman, John Carlos Rowe none at all. Only F. O. Matthiessen, Roy Harvey Pearce, Harold Bloom, Joseph N. Riddel, and Donald Pease have, in their own individually masterful ways, made Whitman a canonical figure (one of many) in their respective theses about American literary history. And despite their excellent readings, in full-length analyses of Whitman's poetry, their names rarely appear. It would seem that a comprehensive appreciation of *Leaves of Grass* precludes theory, and an inclusive theory of American literature excludes Whitman or minimizes the poet's participation in it.

Not only in the established readings by Whitman scholars and among the esoteric polemics of speculative Americanists does Whitman seem to have little theoretical pertinence. He also holds an *a*theoretical, and entirely paradoxical, place in popular conceptions of American literary history. Universally considered America's first great original poet, he is, at the same time, cast in the role of pupil or as the leading disciple of New England's seminal thinker—Emerson. According to many chronologies and surveys of American literature and culture, as the valedictorian of the Orphic school of poetry (outlined in Emerson's essays "The Poet" and "Self-Reliance," and the conclusion of *Nature*), Whitman puts into practice Emerson's vatic pronouncements concerning poetry, prophecy, and power, and becomes the national "singer" envisioned and awaited by the sage, the cultural liberator freeing the New World from its persistent dependence upon archaic forms and contents. To Emerson's beleaguered lament "I look in vain for the poet whom I describe" ("The Poet"), Whitman answers by writing "Song of Myself" and then declares, in an anonymous self-review, "An American bard at last!" (*In Re*, 13). To Emerson's famous congratulatory letter, Whitman responds by printing it (without asking permission) and adding his own infamous and fawning rejoinder in the second edition, even addressing Emerson as "Master" and saying, "These shores you found. I say you have led The States there—have led Me there" (*LGCRE*, 739). As Whitman said in an oft-quoted remark to John Trowbridge in May, 1856, the poet was the "simmering" raw material brought to a "boil" by Emerson's activating flame.[1] Emerson presented Whitman with a philosophy of life and a politics of expression that would shape and direct his visionary energies, a vivifying theory that would transform the immoderate hack journalist into America's pioneer poet. The underlying assumption in this reading is that Whitman had no substantial poetics of his own, that the aspiring ephebe required a preformed theory in order to become a practicing poet.

However, in the last ten years, starting with the publication of C. Carroll Hollis' *Language and Style in "Leaves of Grass,"* Whitman scholarship has managed to gather together into an impressive body of work the special expertise of Whitman scholars, the speculative rigor of Americanist theory, and the sweeping background knowledge of American literary historians. Books and essays by Hollis, M. Wynn Thomas, Betsy Erkkila, Kerry Larson, James Perrin Warren, Harold Aspiz, M. Jimmie Killingsworth, and Eve Sedgwick have incorporated their precursors' scrupulous research and theoretical insight into a sustained critique bringing Whitman's poetry to bear upon modern questions of gender, class, sexuality, and communication. Instead of dismissing earlier treatments of Whitman as inadequate, neglectful, or superficial, and thus rendering their own treatments trivial and high-handed, recent Whitman criticism has built upon previous work to provide new and challenging readings of the poetry. It has taken historical evidence and placed it in the light of contemporary critical debate to highlight crucial problems posed by the poems.

For example, Killingsworth asks how feminist social historians' discussions of "sexual politics" and "the body" affect our interpretation of the *Calamus* poems (and how *Calamus* alters our understanding of "sexual politics" and "the body"). Erkkila politicizes earlier psychological criti-

---

1. John T. Trowbridge, *My Own Story, with Recollections of Noted Persons* (Boston, 1904), 367.

cism by examining "the ways the signs of personal neurosis and crisis we find in his poems are linked with disruptions and dislocations in the political economy." And Thomas "materializes" previous historical research by relating it to the socioeconomic order in Brooklyn in the 1850s and after, especially to the "rapidly disappearing phase of capitalist endeavor" called "artisanship."[2] If criticism were to do differently, it would both ignore the important achievements of nontheoretical Whitman studies and non-Whitmanian theoretical studies and misconstrue their respective aims. It would also ignore the poet's own complex relation to theory, his characterization of theory being any cold, calculating, unfeeling method of analysis such as that used by the "learn'd astronomer." Strangely enough, though he loved to have others talk about his "pomes," Whitman would not have been overly concerned by the scarcity of theoretical analyses of his work.

True to his genuinely American anti-intellectualism, Whitman always maintained an attitude of distrust toward theory. Any conceptual discipline that required formal training or that abandoned "Life immense in passion, pulse, and power" ("One's Self I Sing") he considered a disastrous impoverishment of human nature. From his political perspective, he regarded logic, speculation, aesthetics, or any other theoretical discourse as an elitist practice available only to a select class of sophisticated literati and navel-gazing philosophers, disdainful and decadent personalities hostile to the communal spirit of democracy. Their academic and unemotional terminology marked a sterilizing disengagement from the real world and its political and social struggles, and lent itself to sophistry and rhetoric that compromised and toyed with Justice, Equality, and Patriotic Duty. The spectacle of "limber-tongued lawyers, very fluent but empty feeble old men, professional politicians, dandies, dyspeptics, and so forth" misleading "the solid body of the people" with "Party Platforms, Sections, Creeds" was only the most overt and corrupt political manifestation of a perversely theoretical habit of mind and language.[3] If words and thoughts are fated to relinquish their rightful concrete origin

2. M. Jimmie Killingsworth, *Whitman's Poetry of the Body: Sexuality, Politics, and the Text* (Chapel Hill, N.C., 1989), 96–130; Betsy Erkkila, *Whitman the Political Poet* (New York, 1988), 11; M. Wynn Thomas, *The Lunar Light of Whitman's Poetry* (Cambridge, Mass., 1987), 2.

3. Walt Whitman, *The Eighteenth Presidency!*, ed. Edward F. Grier (Lawrence, Kans., 1956), 19–20, 34.

in human feeling and in the things themselves, and instead refer to dispassionate conceptual inventions with no natural basis, then what becomes not only of Whitman's "physical" poetry but also of those natural self-evident Truths upon which America was formed?

Poetry and Truth would decay into Theory and Ideology, intellectual constructs subject to mutation by lies and rhetoric and other language abuses. So, as many have noted, to counteract the linguistic germ devitalizing America, Whitman sets against the depleted formulae, remote vocabularies, and frigid arguments of critics and academics an organic poetic idiom rife with passionate intensity and grounded in felt existences, purified of poetic diction and heedless of "literary" detail. Renouncing conventional materials and abstract preexistent forms, disdaining theory and its dry-as-dust applications, Whitman tries to render a natural vernacular utterance originating in his heart, inspired by his senses, and expressing his soul. In short, Whitman purports to restore language to its natural, physical, emotive beginnings: herein lies the explanation of Whitman's and his earlier critics' relation to theory.

To qualify as natural, a language must in some way partake in the self-present intuition of feeling and the preinterpretive sense impressions one has (according to this Rousseauist scheme) of real things. Of course, if it were natural, it would not have to "qualify" as anything—it would not *mean* but *be*. Only from an administrative, regulatory position would a natural language have to prove itself as such, and the *predication* of naturality would itself be unnatural. But from Whitman's position, instead of being a simple exterior or posterior record of a primary experience, be it perceptual or emotional, the word must function as a cooperative participant in or an instantaneous manifestation of that experience. It would be potentially itself and its referent, present and future.

In Whitman's case, if the word can be made contiguous or coexistent with the event, the poems would be spontaneously deictic, not distantly representational. Whitman's utterances would spring off the printed page and point readers directly back to *his* here and now, the unique moment of creation, and make it theirs. With a natural idiom acting directly upon readers' infallible instincts (again, to Whitman, it is the intellect that misleads humanity), interpretation becomes superfluous and impertinent, an unnecessary and miscreant intervention of theory and aesthetic distance into the salutary emotive concourse of souls. With *Leaves of Grass* closing the divisive, mediating space opened up by an arbitrary system of signs and a detached reading technique, men and women readers experience the opportunity to pierce their own especial veils of language. By implanting within ordinary communication a poetic idiom that dispenses with the barriers created by intellectual discourse, the exogenous language that diverges from the natural wellsprings of human feeling and that sustains all the other social barriers and class distinctions hindering the progress of democracy, Whitman steers America back to its organic destiny. Or at least that is his intention—by an idiomatic performance to rescue American citizens from a life spent coping with unnatural intermediaries that drain human interaction of its physical energy and undermine its transcendental purpose.

In several of its particulars—an organic conception of language, an Orphic description of the poet, a diatribe against artificiality of form—Whitman's intention echoes many of the prefaces, essays, and treatises making up Romantic aesthetics. And despite his pose as an unschooled "magnificent idler," as a primitive, athletic bard rejecting *literary* inspiration, Whitman was fairly well versed in European literature from the Middle Ages to his own time (see his notes in *NUPM*, V, 1737–1929). Why, then, we might ask, does Whitman's pose hold our attention, and why does his work seem so strikingly innovative and radical? What sets Whitman's version of Romanticism apart from its European forebears is neither its democratic ethos nor its free verse form nor its secular celebration of self nor its affirmation of mutability. Instead, what makes Whitman so important is precisely this: More than any of his contemporaries or precursors, Whitman realizes and contends with the unflagging threat that theory poses to naturality and all the mystifications naturality founds and supports. Through a prodigious insight, Whitman persistently recognizes how theory, with its intellectual modes of discourse, exposes the representational distance and difference "spontaneous" Orphic expression seeks to disguise. He sees how theory explores the arbitrary, conventional basis of putatively organic or symbolic language, and how theory undoes immediacy and deixis, organicism and any linguistic motivation.

Whitman wishes to regard representation, or at least the right kind of representation, as a solution, as an answer to the personal call he awakens to in the early 1850s and as a seminal catalyst in America's ongoing "evolution." But theory intervenes in this progressive or expressive linguistic design and instead converts representation per se into a "problem," a precarious activity necessitating interrogation before action. Representation comes to be seen as problematic when theory brackets metaphysical, ahistorical notions of reality (nature, history, consciousness, and so on) and rigorously analyzes the unit of reality's representation, the sign. If the sign is seen to bear supplementary properties that cannot be said to belong properly to its referent, then the sign can no longer be considered a reliable, transparent vehicle or reflection of the real world. If the sign behaves not simply as an innocuous stand-in, but instead effects transformations upon its natural origin, then our feelings, our perceptions, our ideas, our "truths" become implicated in a volatile, suspect linguistic play. At that point, we can no longer look at language representationally, that is, as a group of signs bound to nature. We must regard language semiotically, that is, as a system of reference made up of signs bound to each other.

This raises the question of what governs communication and constitutes truth. In the former case, true communication rests upon its correspondence to nature; objects and feelings constrain us to be accurate, to be faithful to them and tell the truth, to be sincere. Therefore, for the poet, the task is to find the right representations, the most transparent expressions of self. But in the latter case, with no extralinguistic nature or self to appeal to, communication has no other basis but a social one, and truth is a result of endless conversation and negotiation. If language is not somehow anchored in nature, the sign may still represent, in some recognizable communication system, an object to an interpreter; but in so doing it submits that object to a representational framework with rules of its own (conventional, not natural) and to another person with desires of his or her own. Truth becomes a matter of how others understand those rules, whether they recognize those conventions and accept what they say.

This is the danger of semiosis. It incorporates interpretation into representation, a volatile behavior into a simple correspondence. Words become not the medium of truth, but the pieces people play social games with. Human experience loses its sensible and spiritual purity as it is structured by grammar, temporalized by tense, and parceled out in conjugations and syntax and linguistic redundancy, the preconditions of communication. In actual practice, communication (including poetry) becomes an unpredictable chain of idiosyncratic responses, not a smooth transport of content from self to self. The all-important questions then are: Though incompatible, can the laws of language follow the laws of thought and feeling? and, What is involved in thinking of the word's "open road" as an "infinite semiosis," as an endless dispersal of interpretations?

Rather than functioning to help settle these questions, the sign, loosened from strict referential restraint by theoretical discourse, no longer acts unambiguously as evidence of what is or was or as a vector of truth, but instead becomes a tool of rhetoric. Ideally (or real-ly), one would have recourse to a fixed truth, a self-evident observation that measured a discourse's errancy; but theoretically, one would realize that truth and observation were themselves linguistic constructs liable to the very permutations, translations, and interpretations they would seek to regulate.

Obviously, the last thing Whitman wants is for his favored form of presence—pure, unadulterated feeling—to be violated by the untrustworthy, estranging sign, or for his privileged mode of poetry—spontaneous, oracular utterance—to break down into conventional articulation and "sickly abstractions" (*PW*, I, 295). To render feeling in a decadent literary fashion and to subject it to inimical intellectual analysis would betray "the *bona fide* spirit and relations, from author to reader" (*PW*, I, 293) that produce the ardent interchange of feeling that is the end of great democratic literature. Whitman's task is to actualize this Emersonian compact, to bring the ideal communion out of its propositional form in the essay and live it again and again in poetry.

But theoretical criticism maintains the propositional (or positional) status of all statements, poetic or otherwise, claiming that every proposition has its suppositions. Fastening upon first principles (call them reifications, nostalgia, wish-fulfillments, and so on), theoretical critics ask first what interests are served by any set of beliefs, what intellectual system it derives from, what contradictions or inconsistencies it contains. Theory never gets beyond analysis and dissolution, for theorists always paraphrase affirmations "in the optative mood" (Emerson) and leave poets in "manhood's pondering repose of If" (Melville), the conditional suspension of resolution and advance. They deny any absolute proposition, a preintellectual starting point from which to mount a poetics or a philosophy that could transcend all contingencies.

Always remaining mindful of his poetic ambition, Whitman acutely senses the shadow of theory and its subversive portents, its reduction of truth and feeling to interestedness and discourse. So, neutralizing theory's sabotaging tendencies and relegating the problematics of representation exposed by theory to mere abuses of representation are the opening gestures of Whitman's poetics. Although he ostensibly grounds his project in the positive attempt to found a language adequate to the unaffected American self, his affirmative proposals manifest themselves in practice in the poet's taking a negative, hostile position against theory. To invent a speech that, even in print, transparently presents pure, immediate experience, and to bequeath it to others innocently, Whitman must first disabuse readers of their theoretical habits of mind.

The subject of this book is precisely how that strategy unfolds from 1850 to 1860. It recounts how Whitman's poetics begins in certain biographical events remembered in various essays, diaries, and notebooks, how it develops through his first efforts to publicize an organic American idiom (in the compositions of 1855), and how it is frustrated, initially in his confronting questions of readership and reception (in the 1856 edition), and finally when he is forced to reread and revise his own poetry and to abandon his original poetics (in 1860).

The story told here is one of decline, of the failure of a poetics in execution, of an antitheory undone by performance. The case of Whitman presents readers with a narrative informed by the "resistance to theory" gradually giving way to its anxieties and raising the same problems it sought to repress, thus resulting in the "triumph of theory."[4] It makes little difference that, up until 1860, when he expressly signals the end of his "language experiment," Whitman raises problematic poetic-linguistic issues only in order to refute the "linguists and contenders" ("Song of Myself," l. 80) harassing "natural sayers" (Emerson) and to cast out accidental linguistic properties and effects. For not only doth the poet protest too much but, because he simply says "Nay!" to the theorist's "Yea!" and thereby accepts the latter's terms and conditions and *formally* makes the same argument, Whitman's denial acts more as a repetition of than an escape from theory.

My thesis is that although Whitman's guiding intention is to overcome language, to fend off the possibility that words bear properties that cannot be reduced to human experience, the individual poems and pieces of criticism springing from that Orphic intention nevertheless register its dismemberment. Although testifying to their natural origins and workings, Whitman's writings also declare themselves as instances of failing

4. Paul de Man, *The Resistance to Theory* (Minneapolis, 1986); J. Hillis Miller, "The Triumph of Theory, the Resistance to Reading, and the Question of the Material Base," *PMLA*, CII (1987), 281–92.

resistance to linguistic play, as moments whereby unified utterance disintegrates into a plurality of "clews," "hints," and fugitive "meanings." A close reading of the major poems shows that the more Whitman insists upon his language's organic basis, the more a semiotic vocabulary creeps into his poems, and the more the critic runs up against a display of traces and fragments requiring an active, suppositional interpretation. This dispersion is incomprehensible, for the poet has no instrument to recuperate his or her meandering "meanings" but the original cause of dissemination, language itself.

Whitman realizes this when he tries to develop his naïve conception of the natural bard into a realistic practice. The visionary poetics begins to collapse when Whitman attempts to enter the world as the American Orpheus and then undergoes a frustrating reversal. Instead of singing indigenous lyrics tallying his organic prescriptions, the poet finds himself having to negotiate with all the textual machinations involved in spreading his word. First, he must engage in writing—converting the inarticulate speech of the heart into conventional notation, into alphabetic scripts and diacritical marks and blank white spaces that work accessory transformations upon their original. Second, he must organize publication—constituting natural utterance into a commodity, a unit of mass production measured out by the economic determinations of booksellers and the fickle estimations of public taste. Next, he must endure reading and interpretation—being held up to criticism, subjected to the vanity and prejudice of reviewers and editors, many of whom remain strangely untouched by the oracular tongue that should exercise universal appeal. And last, he must revise. In the process of bringing out new editions, Whitman rereads his past pronouncements and discovers their inadequacy to his present condition, understanding that they were temporarily satisfying but utterly transient "talking cures" whose proper emotive effects could be restored only by a tremulous reconstruction, a process that quickly degenerates into mere habit and reiteration.

These setbacks are not simply the incidental products of a particularly depressing historical situation for an American Romantic poet. Even if Whitman had not had to combat provincial literary tastes, to find other means of support than the meager receipts from book sales, and to cope with his own stifling fits of melancholy, the social and technical pitfalls of being a published poet would not have disappeared. The traps and frustrations of writing, publication, distribution, and reception bring to the foreground not only local conditions but also, and more damagingly to Whitman's poetics, a universal condition of communication—semiosis, the perpetual Protean metamorphosis of the sign.

Easily overlooked in other, less mediated linguistic events such as hearing onself speak in an interior monologue or listening with rapt attention to a spellbinding orator, semiosis abruptly emerges as a dangerous crossing once the intimate presence of bard to votary is disrupted and the printed page intervenes in their mutual awareness. Once the circle of souls is broken, Whitman's initial inspiration must undergo consecutive translations and interpretations, governed only by the slippery law of convention, before it arrives at its rightful harbor, the reader's inner life.

If the sign deviated from its intentional pathway for historical or circumstantial reasons, then preserving the sign's proper function would remain a viable possibility, one resting on the power of primal namers who uphold language's natural purpose. In that case, to shield language from abuse, whether it takes the form of prescription by grammarians and schoolmasters or catachresis by foppish sophisticates, self-appointed guardian poets such as Whitman would take it upon themselves to mark the dividing line between natural and unnatural usage, to purge the latter from social discourse, and to castigate those who foment it. Hence Whitman utters frequent diatribes against the "smart writers and verbal fops" (*NUPM*, II, 898), the "esteemed umpires of taste" (Emerson) who measure enunciation by its refinement and decorum.

But despite the virulence and urgency of Whitman's attacks, they fail to protect natural utterance from perversion and misuse; indeed, their persistence signifies their ineffectiveness. The real danger comes from within, not from without language. It is not only perverse desires or abusive egos but also, and more devastatingly, semiosis, the arbitrary substitution of signs, that undermines natural expression and communication. Viewed from the uncritical perspective Whitman would like to adopt, this linguistic property or force of semiosis renders the proposed natural exchange of heartfelt feeling a tenuous system of sign exchange. But from a critical perspective, language, instead of being a secondary perversion of naturality, presents itself as the constitutive element of naturality. That is, in contrast to a naïve metaphysics, theoretical criticism defines naturality as a secondary construction achieved by a negation of language, its "original."

The actual target of Whitman's jeremiad against corrupt intellectual

11

usage is the linguistic play that facilitates corruption and sets purity up as merely a human invention, not a natural essence. In the poetry, where Whitman is less polemical, his argument is more precise: the fundamental thrust of the first three editions is to protect language from language, to defend the *Leaves* from any incursions of arbitrary semiosis in writing or reading that might disrupt the word's trouble-free representation of human feeling. In order to exemplify and to safeguard this antilinguistic notion of language as a simple harbinger of feeling, Whitman tries to write poems that embody the original feelings they transport. Uncertain of whether feeling might not retain its purity during transmission, of whether embodiment and transport might not yield transformation and disfiguration, Whitman begins to compose a writing against itself, a writing that promotes the unwritten, what cannot be written. In other words, Whitman initiates in *Leaves of Grass* a poetic project whose goal is, paradoxically, to nullify language, whose various affirmations and celebrations of self and nature are, in fact, antithetical reactions to linguistic effects.

For example, Whitman's organicism, which postulates a return to the primal significance of sound, is actually a calculated response to arbitrariness. From an organic perspective, arbitrariness threatens the poet's creative endeavors when the language at his disposal seems to have no concrete sensible signification, when the natural bond of word and thing no longer holds. Creativity then becomes a matter of making new arrangements of preexisting lexicons; invention penetrates no further than language's tropological artifice; and inspiration, originating in some sacred interior, has no adequate outlet.

To take another brief example, Whitman's notion of originality, grounded in the American poet's Adamic self-reliance, is actually a suppression of, and therefore a reliance upon, semiosis. From an Orphic perspective, semiosis threatens the poet when, while composing, he finds himself drawn to prior poems, to other poets' rhythms and diction and imagery, and recognizes that his own originality is a borrowing, a kind of quotation. Poetry then becomes a matter of translation, not of inspiration: it is a question of reforming a precursor's language into one's own image, not of creating a unique language befitting the individual soul.

Semiosis also menaces the poetics when readers scrutinize the poems critically, paraphrasing the poems' emotive content into prosaic discourse and tearing it from its corporeal exterior—the poem as it is. Reading becomes a cerebral process of sign substitution, of trading the pure language of feeling for an aesthetic or philosophical or ethical terminology Whitman would find irrelevant. Under semiosis, wherein the sign is ceaselessly in transit, language comes to operate in both composition and interpretation independently of its proper locus, the soul in feeling and the body in sensation.

This is the inaugural conflict of Whitman's poetics—to express a self, to socialize one's private desires and experiences in such a way that the instrument of revelation, poetic language, remains securely within the purview of its inception. Whitman struggles to achieve an inarticulate utterance, a natural idiom purified of linguistic variance. He pursues a nonmethod that banishes technique (and its accompanying theory) from the creative moment. The fact that Whitman eventually surrenders to the contradictions of his metaphysics and acknowledges his poetics' impracticality does not change the fact that his nostalgic ambitions carry him through dozens of now canonical poems. Though frustrated and delayed, the hope of writing the American vernacular idiom is nevertheless a prolific one. How to do so, how to reify an ideal language possessing neither an extraneous past nor an extravagant future, is the question shaping Whitman's most productive years (1855–1860), the dilemma the most interesting poems attempt to resolve. Contrary to Whitman's expectations, those poems prove to be the site where language turns upon his intentions and resists his own resistance to language, but this in no way devalues the poems.

The course of Whitman's resistance and its overcoming begins with certain experiences he had in early manhood and middle age, real-life events that seemed to confirm the possibility of an unmediated or organically mediated contact of souls. These included listening to Emerson lecture in 1842, attending Italian opera in New York in the 1840s and 1850s, hearing Edward Thompson Taylor preach in Boston in 1860, and random "physiognomic" communions the poet silently shared with casual "promenaders" and ferry passengers. In such experiences, Whitman believed he had absorbed the living presence of another being, that two souls had harmonized in a self-effacing medium transcending language. Whitman's reinterpretation of those memories and his speculations as to how those experiences could be enacted in poetry are the subject of the following chapter. It focuses on a gathering of the poet's tentative explorations of various forms of communication—"vocalization," "physiognomy," phrenology, phonetic script, and so on—and proposes to outline and analyze Whitman's search for an order of signs concordant with the soul.

Following that, this chronicle of Whitman's "language experiment" continues with the first edition, mainly "Song of Myself," analyzing the particular linguistic dilemma he now encounters—the problematics of writing. For the moment taking for granted the unmediated character of certain real-life occurrences, we see that, in trying to represent or reenact them in poetry, Whitman now faces the predicament of composing with pen and paper an experience of feeling-exchange that rests upon the palpable presence of all participants and their mutual recognition of a natural medium. Obviously, there is no getting around the "printed and bound book" ("Song of Myself," l. 1088); but if Whitman can shape his verse along the lines of a genesis and structure matching nature's, then the hazards of inscription can be minimized. If he can write a natural text that reproduces without depleting or supplementing nature's meaningfull energies, then the chance of misinterpretation or in*aff*ectiveness lessens to negligibility.

Whitman's egotistical epic relentlessly pursues this nostalgia—all the while, however, raising the specter of the failure to communicate (this is the point where Whitman himself becomes a theorist). The productive tensions and contradictions in "Song of Myself" come from precisely this struggle between naturality and language, creativity and criticism, inspiration and composition, the latter constantly making inroads upon the former. Endlessly seeking ways to fix and determine the sign's rogue operations, futilely coping with ubiquitous linguistic obstructions, Whitman makes that conflict the raw material of his art, casts his agonistic poetics and poetry as the subject of the poem, and then offers no resolution, preferring to leave the issue in an ambiguous, probationary state.

Even if Whitman were successful in composing a natural poem, still a problem would remain, namely, interpretation. Composing a natural language presents the poet with a series of impediments and frustrations that a truly inspired visionary bard may or may not overcome, but controlling that language's reception introduces him to an altogether different set of problems and pratfalls. In Whitman's case, after the publication of the 1855 edition, he finds he must accept the prospect that his apotheosis of an American idiom, his revolutionary verse form, and his revivification of literary language have little control over the capricious vicissitudes of reader response. The utterly contrary and miscellaneous replies to the 1855 edition, reactions ranging from unreserved acclaim to scurrilous ridicule, demonstrate to him that natural writing is a necessary but insufficient condition of communion. To ensure the proper concourse of souls, Whitman realizes, he must also inculcate natural reading—a compliant, receptive attitude that takes the written sign as a physical presence to be felt, not a detached, insubstantial trace to be interpreted.

This is the critical thrust of the 1856 edition. In it, Whitman counsels readers in how to read his poems, how to dispense with their cultivated scholarly, aesthetic, and intellectual habits and to imbibe the volume's satiating, enlivening "speech of the proud and melancholy races and of all races who aspire" (PW, II, 457). It is the resistance to theory transformed into the resistance to reading, the fear of language sharpened into the fear of misinterpretation.

That resistance collapses in 1860, the third edition, which brings us to the end of Whitman's experimental poetics. It ends when Whitman, upon rereading his earlier poems and finding them inadequate to his present condition, revises and reorganizes them for further publication. In his attempt to improve and update his book, Whitman violates the supposedly universal, irrefutable, and immutable language of his heart, and commits the pure emotive idiom to calculated editorial amendment. By performing this self-revision, Whitman positions his creations squarely within the semiotic sequence of translations, quotations, displacements, and reinterpretations that he intended his language to halt. As a result, he relinquishes his grandiose bardic posture and regretfully acknowledges the sign's sovereignty.

This turn of events is dramatized in the two major poems added in 1860. In "As I Ebb'd with the Ocean of Life," the poet laments the estrangement he feels when scanning his previous utterances, the shock and despair of encountering a self no longer identical to his own. In "Out of the Cradle Endlessly Rocking," Whitman stages in a triple perspective (bird-boy-poet) the semiotic predicament characterizing the poet's activity, the lapse of originality into quotation, expression into articulation, feeling into interpretation. In these Sea-Drift lyrics, the nostalgia for a natural language gives way to a demystified awareness of the linguistic "origins" of "man" and "nature."

Whitman's antitheoretical proviso runs its course in the six years preceding the Civil War, eventually succumbing to its inherent contradictions and emerging as a complex theoretical enterprise in its own right. But interpretations of Whitman's poetry must still contend with its resistances and come to terms with the implications those resistances have for criticism per se. In the sense that it raises questions of the word's adequacy to a given state of affairs, questions of mimesis, representation, interpretation, and so on, and that it challenges the self-enclosed unity of creative vision and emotive response, Whitman's poetry and poetics is an investigation into the theory and practice of criticism. It embroils all practices of explication and its aims—to expose the text, to lay bare its historical and psychological foundations, to unveil its "truth"—within the poetry's own textual assertions and equivocations.

The poet anticipates theoretical analysis by posing, inversely, the same linguistic dilemmas and ambiguities that theory seeks to uncover in literary texts. Criticism of Whitman's writing, therefore, is a secondary, derivative experiment, an ambivalent, uncertain rewriting wavering between repeating the life of another text and sacrificing its progenitor to come into its own. Like all theoretical criticism, which knows that criticism can never be a simple opening introduction or closing index to its prolific centerpiece, this book is an examination of originality and secondariness, transparency and translation, repetition and supplementation, in poetry and criticism, in Whitman's poetry and Whitman's criticism. It is a "backward glance" at priority, a conscious rumination upon spontaneous expression, one whose failure or success depends not so much on its accuracy or exposition or fidelity as on the rigor and self-consciousness with which it addresses those metaphysical questions in the context of *Leaves of Grass*.

1
Theory

When writing the books and articles that they hoped would secure Whitman's enduring fame and protect him from literary enemies, the "Whitmaniacs," as they were called (mainly, William Douglas O'Connor, John Burroughs, Richard Maurice Bucke, William Sloane Kennedy, and Horace Traubel), insisted upon characterizing *Leaves of Grass* as the natural, spontaneous utterance of a passionate, primitive soul. Kennedy typifies their high conception of Whitman's Adamic art when he writes, "It is precisely the most difficult thing in the world for a poet or painter to imitate nature's spontaneity." He further asserts, "The style of the poem will flow spontaneously and in original forms from noble aim and passion." Even a less favorable reviewer like Charles A. Dana, in the first known notice of *Leaves of Grass*, had to admit that "his words might have passed between Adam and Eve in Paradise, before the want of fig-leaves brought no shame."[1]

Leaves of Grass substantiates these claims, as Whitman's defenders never tired of informing us. They praised Whitman's avoidance of artifice and ornamentation and any literary techniques that, they thought, only served to vitiate inspiration. They were exhilarated by the natural rhythms of *Leaves of Grass*. Although standard versification prescribed artificial limits to the expression of feeling, Whitman's free, open verse, guided by his unpredictable moods and varied impressions, renounced any strictly

1. William Sloane Kennedy, *Reminiscences of Walt Whitman* (London, 1896), 162–63; Charles A. Dana, Review of Walt Whitman's *Leaves of Grass*, in *Walt Whitman: The Critical Heritage*, ed. Milton Hindus (London, 1971), 23.

literary restraints whatsoever. They applauded the pristine, joyful cama-raderie Whitman dramatized in his poetry and celebrated in his prose as a utopian alternative to the literary elitism and social hierarchies that kept men apart. In other words, Whitman's most vocal admirers were impressed not so much by the quality of his ideas or his mastery of form and language as they were excited by what they assumed to be his natu-ral genius for expressing pure feeling without restriction or mediation.

Whitman was pleased to have his poems hailed as natural and immedi-ate, for the favorable critics' judgment confirmed the success of the poetic project as he had imagined it at the beginning of his "great career." In an early notebook (1855–1860?), Whitman writes, "The office of the poet is to remove what stands in the way of our perceiving the beauty and per-fection" (*NUPM*, I, 147). That is, the poet is to clear the ground, to dis-pose of that which hinders the direct revelation of "beauty." Because they exacerbate the difficulty of disclosing feeling, obstructions such as liter-ary allusions, elaborate metaphors, inverted syntax, poetic diction, and so on, are to be excluded from composition.

In *Specimen Days,* he says, "Nature seems to look on all fixed-up po-etry and art as something almost impertinent" (*PW*, I, 293). In other words, a self-consciously literary style—"fixed-up poetry"—needlessly and arrogantly supervenes a layer of artifice onto an already perfect order and frustrates the desire for immediacy. To avoid such a self-defeating technique, the poet must, as Whitman writes in his "Rules for Composi-tion" (a manuscript fragment), opt for "a perfectly transparent plate-glassy style, artless, with no ornaments" (*NUPM*, I, 101) in order to unveil the "perfection" heretofore concealed, the feeling previously re-pressed. Whether or not the epithets "transparent style" and "artless technique" are oxymorons and whether "beauty" might not lie just as much in the "ornament" as in the thing or feeling itself are questions Whitman here neglects to address. Considering the poet's jealous reac-tions regarding opinions of his poetry, the implication is that a faithful critic should do the same.

The conception of Whitman's poetry as unmediated emotion, however, leaves the critic with little else to say. Certainly candid emotion requires no interpretation; it just *is*. Beyond signification, it does not mean; it does. It is performative, emotive (*ex-* "out of" + *movere* "to move"). In fact, any verbal elaboration of the emotions in Whitman's poetry would be a gratuitous supplementation of what is already complete and frank.

Interpretation would suggest that the expression were somehow deficient, that only under the direction of critical arguments could one experience the poetry properly. But that intellectual mediation would disrupt the poems' emotional forcefulness and thus annul Whitman's primary goal. Also, as Whitman's devotees avowed, the pure and integral feeling at the core of *Leaves of Grass* needed no explanation (even though they spent much of their careers writing defenses of the bard). Readers could be invigorated with the healthful feelings of his songs without the assistance of critics.

How, then, is one to be a responsible critic of Whitman's poetry? Can one perform an analytical interpretation of his canon, or does the belief that his poetry needs no critical exegesis compel one into *ad hominem* exaltations of the Orphic and visionary literatus while apologetically explaining away one's own intellectual formulations? Whitman's admirers seem to find criticism adventitious and even exaltation almost tautologous in the face of the poems' self-exaltations. After having extolled the poet at length, they often found themselves somewhat disarmed when they turned to the poetry. On occasion, they would even turn their manuscripts over to Whitman so that the poet might write their criticism for them.[2]

For this reason, early criticism of Whitman reads like a New Critic's nightmare. Bucke spends less than a quarter of "his" book analyzing the poems. Burroughs, in his second book on Whitman, confines his study to relating thematic issues to the poet himself. Only the last twenty pages of Kennedy's book make an attempt to examine Whitman's language for its poetic qualities. And even Whitman's favorite piece of criticism, the Frenchman Gabriel Sarrazin's "Walt Whitman," does little more than quote long passages from the poetry and offer brief metaphysical paraphrases and acclaim for the poet.[3]

Whitman's critics hesitated to analyze Whitman's language because they thought their words inadequately rendered what they sensed intuitively in his words—an indescribable potency, a natural force that appealed to feeling, not intellect, a vague something that analysis could not penetrate. Bucke admits that "the ideas expressed [in *Leaves of Grass*]

2. See, *e.g.*, Stephan Railton, ed., *Walt Whitman's Autograph Revisions of the Analysis of "Leaves of Grass" (For Dr. R. M. Bucke's "Walt Whitman")* (New York, 1974), text notes, along with the introductory essay by Quentin Anderson.
3. Gabriel Sarrazin, "Walt Whitman," trans. Harrison S. Morris, in *In Re*, 159–94.

are of scarcely any value or importance compared with the passion, the never-flagging emotion, which is in every line, almost in every word, and which cannot be set forth or even touched by commentary." Whitman's poetry, then, comprised more of passions than words, stands on its own merits and is beyond interpretation or even apology. Criticism only etiolates poetry's emotive essence. Burroughs echoes Bucke's idea that "commentary" on Whitman's work always proves wanting when he concludes his book by confessing, "The main thing I wanted to say about him I have not said, cannot say: the best about him cannot be told anyway" (Burroughs significantly groups Whitman, his ideas, and his poems together in the pronoun "him").[4]

Whitman himself was the first to foster the notion that "telling" or commenting somehow seemed superfluous or even destructive to understanding his poetry. "The poetry of the future," he writes, extolling his own work as futural, "aims at the free expression of emotion and to arouse and initiate, more than to define or finish" (*PW*, II, 481). To "define or finish," to affix semantic laws and logical support to the "free expression of emotion," would be to domesticate and trivialize Whitman's initial spontaneous impulse.

"Finishing" would also, in a larger context, impoverish human relations, poetry being but one of the more profound forms of human contact. But to "arouse and initiate" the emotions of the reader in sympathy with one's own aroused emotions would strengthen and ennoble human relations. To Whitman and his followers, a shared, inarticulate emotion bonds women and men together far more intensively than standard legal or political communication. When souls make contact, words are unnecessary. Indeed, more often than not, they frustrate genuine contact, for Whitman thinks of words as slipping too easily into the false and unnatural and corrupt. Words tend to channel emotion into what the poet regarded as alienating creeds and inhuman disciplines, the very disposition Whitman seeks to curtail.

Therefore, in order to facilitate a yearning soul's desire to exert a magnetic charm over other souls without the interposition of lifeless social forms, including language, Whitman tries to compose a style and a structure whose provisionally intervening words melt away in the ultimate primal embrace. As an anonymous reviewer of the time puts it, "His

4. Richard Maurice Bucke, *Walt Whitman* (Philadelphia, 1883), 159; John Burroughs, *Whitman: A Study* (Boston, 1896), 263.

writings, bare of ornament, devoid of the verbal graces by which the author is more often concealed than expressed, produce the effect of a mental nudity" (*In Re*, 98–99; quoted by Burroughs without citation).

But if one chooses to interpret Whitman's poetry as "mental nudity"—that is, as unmediated emotion precluding interpretation—one must somehow explain away the mediating signs that occasionally appear in the poems. One must not only discount the fact that Whitman's poems are made of signs, but also must ignore the numerous moments when Whitman explicitly calls attention to his protagonists' encounters with signs and their resulting predicament. He frequently employs the word "sign" or its equivalent ("word," "type," "symbol," "clew," "hint," "mark," and so on), sometimes at crucial dramatic occasions, often making the poem's outcome rest upon how that sign is read. "Out of the Cradle Endlessly Rocking" culminates in "the sea" revealing to the boy "the word final, superior to all." "As I Ebb'd with the Ocean of Life," originally published in *Atlantic Monthly* (April, 1860) as "Bardic Symbols," begins with the poet wandering along the shore "seeking types." In "When I Read the Book," Whitman calls his knowledge of his "real life" "a few diffused faint clews and indirections." And in "Song of Myself," when a child asks the poet, "What is the grass?"—a significant question, considering the book's title—Whitman says, among other things, "I guess it is a uniform hieroglyphic" (l. 103).[5]

Other examples of explicit signs, and signs of signs or words signifying words, abound in Whitman's canon. Given the abundance of terms denoting mediation, how could Whitman and his contemporaries grant the poems unmediated status? How could they see his language as natural, spontaneous utterance permitting readers ecstatic emotional experiences when the poetry contained words that denied its immediacy and screened its emotive core? What desire motivates Whitman's votaries, following the master's example, either to disregard or to reassert the contradiction? What rationale allows Whitman to cover it up?

The answer lies in Whitman's general attitude toward language and

---

5. All quotations are taken from the *Variorum* edition of *Leaves of Grass*. Except where indicated otherwise, I quote the earliest version of each poem. However, line numbers are given for the last version of each poem, causing some discrepancy in citation. Any major changes in the poem, such as lines deleted or added or rearranged, will be noted parenthetically after the line number citation. To see how a poem or section evolved over the years, consult the *Variorum*.

how it leads to the particular kinds of signs he singles out for his readers to appreciate. Although Whitman never outlined a coherent theory of language, he did maintain an abiding obsession with the subject. Although the evidence is scattered, one can still compile a large body of remarks on language dating from the mid-1850s up until his death in 1892. Dozens of manuscript fragments, a lengthy oration (never delivered) on the American idiom, lists of words and observations on etymology in a notebook apparently intended for a dictionary, essays on his favorite public speakers, notes on oratory copied out of popular textbooks, articles on slang and usage, articles on literature, and telling statements about "words" sprinkled throughout the poetry, all comprise Whitman's meandering but illuminating ideas about language. Although his linguistic postulates and speculations do not amount to a developed theory, they do outline an embryonic poetics, a literary design that, although drifting into contradiction and ambivalence, manifests a large-scale intention at work.

A comprehensive study of Whitman's linguistic premises and conclusions reveals a curious bifurcation in his opinions. On the one hand, Whitman aggrandizes language. He attributes to words spiritual and mesmerizing powers: "Nothing is more spiritual than words" (*DN*, III, 730); "There is an endless, indefinable, tantalizing charm in words" (*NUPM*, V, 1626).[6] He postulates an organic connection between word and thing—"A perfect user of words uses things" (*DN*, III, 729)—and a mimetic or expressive relationship, without distortion, between word and desire—"Language is the mirror of the living inward consciousness"; (*NUPM*, V, 1628); "Every soul has its own individual language" (*NUPM*, I, 60). And Whitman's oft-proclaimed motive for writing *Leaves of Grass* was "to articulate and faithfully express . . . my own physical, emotional, moral, intellectual, and aesthetic Personality" (*PW*, II, 714; note the order of importance implied in this list). He also affirms a natural basis for language: "Language is a living Original. It is not made but

6. This quotation and any others that appear in *NUPM*, V, 1626–62, come from William Swinton's *Rambles Among Words* (New York, 1864), a philological treatise that most scholars agree Whitman had a hand in writing. Grier includes in *NUPM* a brief summary of biographical and stylistic evidence pointing to Whitman's role in its composition. For the fullest treatment of the question, see C. Carroll Hollis, "Whitman and William Swinton: A Cooperative Friendship," *American Literature*, XXX (1959), 425–49; and James Perrin Warren, "Whitman as Ghostwriter: The Case of *Rambles Among Words*," *Walt Whitman Quarterly Review*, II (1984), 22–30.

grows. The growth of language repeats the growth of the plant" (*NUPM*, V, 1627); "Perhaps Language is more like some vast living body" (*PW*, II, 577).

But although he hails language for its natural spirituality, he also condemns language for its wanton artificiality. He attacks poeticisms and "intellectualisms" both to purify language of corrupt usage and to expose the necessary result of stylized verbal expression—the deviation of feeling. Although Whitman at times limits his disdain for words by reproving only perverse "literary" or intellectual practices, at other times he expands his dismissal to all practices. Because he often neglects to distinguish one usage from another, it seems that the problem lies not only in this or that usage, but in the inherent properties of the medium itself. Whitman may expound upon the defects of pedantic grammarians and fastidious critics who rob language of its spirituality and vigor (see *DN*, III, 666–67 and 809–10), but he also believes, according to his friend Helen Price, that "the ardent expression in words of affection often tended to destroy affection."[7] What mere word, he asks, can bear the power of an honest emotion? He approves of how "the young men of these states . . . never give words to their most ardent friendships" (*DN*, III, 741). He ranks "Book-learning" and "Erudition" "low among the glories of humanity" because they reduce self-expression to quotation and mannerism (*NUPM*, I, 322–23) and fail, as Whitman says of his first *Leaves of Grass*, to "express, above all artificial regulation and aid, the eternal bodily composite, cumulative, natural character of one's self" (*PW*, II, 468).

But then he also denies the adequacy of *Leaves of Grass* to embody his "Personality": "before all my arrogant poems the real Me stands yet untouch'd, untold, altogether unreach'd" ("As I Ebb'd"). And in the first Preface, he extends his mistrust of language beyond the poetic sphere to include any kind of articulation: "Who troubles himself about his ornaments or fluency is lost" (*PW*, II, 440); "There is that indescribable freshness and unconsciousness about an illiterate person that humbles and mocks the power of the noblest expressive genius" (*PW*, II, 438).

These contrary examples could be seen to demonstrate a repudiation of traditional, uninspired usages of language and thus to affirm his own untroubled achievement of idiomatic purity. But they also manifest a prob-

7. Cited in Bucke, *Walt Whitman*, 34.

lem Whitman faces in trying to reconcile the mutual historicity and universality, as well as the naturality and instrumentality of language. Along with indicating a concern over influence, Whitman's struggle to secure the organicism and spirituality of words and his discouragement over language's utter extraneousness attest to a broader anxiety about the uses and abuses of language, literary and nonliterary. That is to say, Whitman's alternating testimonial to and depreciation of words evince his dismay—indeed, the dismay of every poet but the first poet, Orpheus— over the arbitrary, conventional nature of ordinary signs. Like his Romantic forebears, Whitman suspects that words, instead of evoking transparently a natural presence, will involve some supplementation that veils their emotive origin.

This age-old suspicion, here Americanized, lies at the center of Whitman's poetics and partly explains the peculiar tensions and prevarications in his poems. Whitman's verbal gestures for and against words amount to a flight from the unpredictable future of communication, a resistance to conventional language and all its extrahuman, unfeeling effects.

Arbitrary conventionalism troubles Whitman because, if there is no natural motivation for the sign, nothing guarantees the sincerity and candor of emotional expression. Without a natural bond between sign and meaning, sign and intention, desire, or referent, emotion must pass through a conventional system of mediations prone to familiarity, cliché, parody, and hypocrisy. Ever subject to institutionalization, language becomes, in Whitman's eyes, an alienating social discourse, "society" being either the one to whom Whitman directs his desires—his mother, his favorite "comrade" at the time, his siblings, the reader—or the culture and tradition that grounds the medium and constitutes "others" as such. In either case, having to convert his desires into a communicable medium in order to satisfy them means that they are no longer entirely his own.

In translating his lawless feelings into a verbal system obeying a necessary but impersonal order, Whitman must oblige the reader to retranslate those signs back into their emotional content, an interpretive process inevitably liable to misconstruction. To ensure that readers follow that natural regression, Whitman publishes anonymous reviews of his own poems, rewrites (often inaccurately) his friends' manuscript biographies and critical articles, casts himself as the martyred "good gray poet," all in a shameless effort to forestall readings of his poetry that fail to correspond with his intentions.

Whitman's twofold attitude toward language, then, embodies contradictory, though equally escapist, methods of obviating arbitrariness, the "cause" of miscommunication. Whitman's exaltation of language denies arbitrariness by attributing to the sign an organic connection with its "object." The unfortunate difference between conventional sign and natural emotion is then dialectically overcome in Whitman's American version of the Romantic symbol, a concrete sensuous image that shares the transcendental properties of the sublime Idea it stands for. In Whitman's phrase, "Words follow character—nativity, independence, individuality" (*DN*, III, 732). The double meaning of the verb "follow" establishes the motivated relation between words and their transcendental origin in that words both conform to subjective laws and issue spontaneously from the self. Ultimately, a natural, not an arbitrary, principle regulates the proper workings of language.

However, a contemporary problem hinders the extrapolation of such an untroubled and uninterrogated principle: that is, through a grand historical mistake, says Whitman, language was transformed from a living agency of feeling into a spurious contrivance of custom and pedantry. Echoing Emerson (who in turn echoes, in the "Language" chapter of *Nature* and in "The Poet," common eighteenth-century theories of language and its origins), Whitman claims that language in its most primitive form consisted of an inspired natural idiom vitally metaphorical yet corresponding uniformly with things. At first material and sensuous, and therefore poetic, words were tropes whose nearness to the essential passions and the concrete world secured their aptness and prevented their corruption. The historical decay Whitman laments throughout his writings on language came about when a moral or conceptual denotation was abstracted from animate metaphors and categorized in intellectural discourse. The mythical language of transparent names became embedded in "fossil poetry" (Emerson's epithet), lost in idle "talk of the beginning and the end," "mockings or arguments," words without solid reference or candor of emotion, "book-words" ("Song of Myself," ll. 38 and 81; "Song of the Banner at Daybreak," l. 9).

Through this intellectualizing catachresis, in which idiom ossifies into abstraction, the figurative basis of conceptual language was forgotten or repressed, perhaps, as Whitman might say with Nietzsche, for reasons of power and institutionalization. Having been torn from the organic matrix of nature, words deteriorated into colorless designations devoid of actual human relevance. A great metaphysical error set in, an erection in human history of an incurable dualism of word and thing. This abstraction of meaning out of the world did not simply make rationality possible; it also made alienation the rule of civilized behavior. Words work no longer in the service of life. They become nihilistic.

And so a dead language prevails in the world. The "dandyism and impotence in literature" (*DN*, III, 740) takes poetry out of the "open air" and encloses it in the effete salon. The "excessively diffuse and impromptu character" of "American oratory" (*NUPM*, VI, 2333) renders the sacred art of speechmaking a theatrical sham. The modern custodians of usage, lexicographers and grammarians, enforce life-draining strictures upon "the living structure of language in its largest sense" (*DN*, III, 810) and make sterile dictionaries and rhetorics the tyrannical repositories of propriety.

To counteract the deadening effects of intellectualization, Whitman continues, to restore "this great thing, the renovated English speech in America" (*DN*, III, 732), and reawaken the metaphorical, emotive energy of words, the poet exemplifies and embodies the necessity of a return to common speech. In ordinary parlance—"the blab of the pave" ("Song of Myself," l. 154)—may be found, he asserts, the natural vitality of an Adamic language reclaimed. Although so-called literature has forsaken its emotive sources and become an instrument of barren erudition and foppishness—"What a poor, indigent, watery affair is our literary expression" (*NUPM*, V, 1661)—the daily conversation of the lower classes, by abiding close to its origin in human labor and desire, has retained its organic character. Not confined to libraries or restricted by decorum, "vulgar" speech and slang diction grow and change according to the real lives of men and women. Because it always appears in conjunction with natural human activities, common speech plays a conspicuous part in the quotidian world Whitman catalogs and commemorates in his poetry.

As he says in a panegyric titled "Slang in America" (1885): "Language, be it remember'd, is not an abstract construction of the learn'd, or of dictionary-makers, but is something arising out of the work, needs, ties, joys, affections, tastes, of long generations of humanity, and has its bases broad and low, close to the ground. Its final decisions are made by the masses, people nearest the concrete, having most to do with actual land and sea" (*PW* II, 573). This conception of language, a conception that devalues the concept, reverses the standard metaphysical alignment of abstraction with universal truth and idiom with shadowy particulars, and yet attempts to reclaim the universal in the particular. As Whitman would have it, any "abstract construction" that elevates language into some ethereal category accessible only to the "learn'd" marks a perverse deviation from "the ground," the human actuality Whitman finds sufficient unto itself. But in the colorful "repartees and impromptus" (*PW*, II, 577) of illiterate boatmen and bus drivers whose company Whitman enjoyed so much lies "the lawless germinal element" (*PW*, II, 572) of a logos of emotion unmediated by tradition or learning. In the mouths of workers, words shed intellectual baggage and regain their materiality and hence their capacity to affect the senses and the soul. That is, they become poetic.

Whitman proposes as his task to translate this vernacular and idiomatic force into a book of poems, to replicate in print the free speech of "the masses" in such a way that nothing vital or concrete gets lost or distorted in the translation. A talent for artistic polish, a scrupulous mastery of technique, a scholarly attitude toward a literary heritage, all falsify the initial inspiration and detract from genuine emotion: "I never think about literary perfection. . . . It is the *man* and the *feeling*" (*Cor*, I, 134; the ellipsis is mine, the italics are Whitman's). Above all, the integrity of simple, honest feeling is to be safeguarded. Abstract philosophy, learning, and literariness constrain feeling, but feeling still survives in the streets, in common everyday speech, and, Whitman hopes, in his poems.

Grounded in the needs and desires of ordinary, ingenuous men and women, the spoken vernacular, condemned by intellectuals as barbarous, springs directly from feeling and promises forthright self-expression. Leaping instantaneously from the heart and the senses, common speech traverses the stay of articulation, the interval of rhetorical calculation whereby a discourse is matched, or mismatched, with feeling. This nearly physiological, almost unconscious language, this idiom of the open road, blithely skips the temporal pause between reception and response that marks the intrusion of convention into nature. So, the poet concludes, because of its intimate, spontaneous relation to life, the vernacular, paradoxically, is the highest language. To the frustration of "dictionary-makers" and men of letters, the power and greatness of language lies in its unstudied, workaday origins. To Whitman, this is a fact he need not argue, for it can be observed irrefutably out there in democratic society. Indeed, argument would only succumb to the very practices Whitman here intends to overcome.

Yet it should be noted that Whitman himself once aspired to writing a dictionary. Starting in the mid-1850s, he began to fill a notebook with lists of words and definitions he copied out of other dictionaries, newspaper and journal clippings on philology, etymology, jargon, printing, and so on, adding his own observations on the English language in the hope that someday he would assemble the authoritative storehouse of the American idiom.[8] Given Whitman's outspoken criticism of grammarians and philologists, one could accuse him of hypocrisy, or of resentfully attacking or denying the merit of those who had succeeded where he, as yet, had failed. (The manuscripts betray a set desire to publish a formal treatise on language, but Whitman never managed to do so.) These are the kind of accusations often made, justifiably, against Whitman during his lifetime.

But in this case, Whitman's attitude toward philologists remained consistent and logical all his life, given his premises, and went far beyond insecurity, for he never intended to become a philologist in the conventional nineteenth-century sense. He sought to study and evaluate language from a different point of view and with a different purpose in mind. That is, in analyzing the English language, Whitman wants to establish a canonical lexicon and syntax that would preserve the native spiritualism in words that standard linguistic taxonomies destroy. Whitman's philological principles differ from the accepted lexicographer's in that the latter classifies and defines words by "rigid grammatical rules," "Morbidness for nice spelling," and, "Dazzled by the lustre of the classical tongues," a preference for "an obedient, elegant and classically handsome tongue dialect" (*DN*, III, 666, 740, 810). Whitman, on the other hand, attempts to delineate "the true broad fluid language of democracy" according to the "wild, intractible suggestive" "genius underneath our speech" (*DN*, III, 809–10).

Rather than reinscribing the meaning of words after they have been tamed by intellectual usage, Whitman wished to circumvent such his-

---

8. William White has edited this notebook and placed it in *DN*, III, 664–727.

torical accretions by investigating etymologies, by "Tracing words to origins" (*DN*, III, 725). In that way he can discover their archetypal naming function. (He also said, *"Language cannot be Traced to First Origins,"* but this is but one contradiction to a nearly unrelenting push toward origins in Whitman's philological writings.[9]) In the process, the poet will render the American idiom in all its primordial vigor and prove that "Language is not a cunning conventionalism arbitrarily agreed upon" (*NUPM*, V, 1652), but instead a living organism responsive to the pulsations of humanity. The assumption is that language lives and breathes within a necessary order just as men and women do: this, in Whitman's view, is the seminal fact that philologists forget.

Whitman's dictionary never came to fruition, nor did he produce any comprehensive argument affirming the natural basis of language. He filed his notes and clippings away, periodically sorting through them to revise them or discuss them with friends and admirers, mainly Traubel, in his declining years. One set of notes, dating probably from the late 1850s, Traubel edited after Whitman's death and published in 1904 under the title *An American Primer*.[10] Originally intended as a public lecture (but never delivered), the *Primer* is Whitman's most sustained attempt to outline the processes and implications of his organic principles. In this exultant, sometimes incoherent little notebook, which F. O. Matthiessen, Charles Feidelson, and other noteworthy Americanists have used to elucidate Whitman's poetics, Whitman expresses his faith in a certain spiritual and emotional fecundity immanent in language, yet latent until the "perfect writer" activates it.

Whitman notes the "strange charm of aboriginal names" (*Pr*, 30) and the "lurking curious charm in the sound of some words" (3). He proclaims the physical energies of words: "A perfect writer would make words sing, dance, kiss, do the male and female act . . . or do anything that man or woman or the natural powers can do" (16). He endows "names" with a nationalistic mission: "I say America, too, shall be com-

9. Emory Holloway and Ralph Adimari, eds., *New York Dissected: A Sheaf of Recently Discovered Newspaper Articles by the Author of "Leaves of Grass"* (New York, 1936), 56.

10. White has also edited *An American Primer* and included it in *DN*, III, but for reasons of simplicity, I mainly use Traubel's edition (Cambridge, Mass., 1904). White's edition contains all of Whitman's deletions and corrections as they appear in the manuscript. Only when Traubel's editorial changes seem unwarranted do I use White's transcript.

memorated—shall stand rooted in the ground in names—and shall flow in the water in names and be suffused in time, in days, in months, in their names" (33). And he appoints words to be the bearers of history: "They are the body of the whole of the past" (7). In less hyperbolic phrasing, language embodies spiritual and material, racial and universal, past and future; it is, in its pure form, the adhesive of democracy.

These grandiose claims for words sound like typical Whitmanian bombast, and one could dismiss them as merely part of the rhetorical fusillade he used in extolling his own poetry. Once again, one could, using a disparaging critical tactic common from Whitman's time to the present, debase his scholarly writings by qualifying them as either thinly concealed narcissistic homage to *Leaves of Grass* or self-indulgent effusions of passion. Even his most sympathetic critics must admit that these writings sometimes sink to embarrassingly bathetic depths, usually when they strain too hard to glorify the mundane.

But apart from the inaptly overblown powers Whitman seems to attribute to words merely for rhetorical or selfish reasons, these exaltations have a logical, that is, metaphysical, basis as well. Whitman's hyperbolic predications of language derive necessarily from the fundamental assumption in *An American Primer*—namely, that language is an organic, motivated extension of what is natural in human life (like Emerson's and Hegel's, Whitman's linguistic presuppositions are grounded firmly in the concept "life" itself). Assertions about the kinetic force and magnetic charm of words arise from a certain logic of the sign, however idiosyncratic, whose first axiom is that the sign is natural, not conventional and factitious. A higher law than arbitrary agreement initiates the moment of signification.

Whitman writes: "Do you think words are positive and original things in themselves?—No: words are not original and arbitrary in themselves.—Words are a result—they are the progeny of what has been or is in vogue" (*Pr,* 8). Although words are not "original in themselves," their secondary nature does not in this instance imply a fall, a lapse from purity. Because they are a "result" of or an accessory to an original presence, a felt but unsignified feeling, words have their proper place in the natural order of things. Words are "progeny" (*pro-* "forth" + *gen-* "birth, race, kind, gender"), the offspring of human desire and the genealogy of human history.

If words were "arbitrary in themselves," if they had no organic connection with nature, they would belong in the same category as fashion, manners, class, and other counterfeit human inventions. Poetry would be measured by its urbanity and refinement, its polished artifice and regular design. The straightforward expression of heartfelt emotion would invariably be labeled vulgar nonpoetry, as Whitman's early poetry was. Without a natural impetus for signmaking, the cooperative relation between private being and public expression would break down, leaving each individual sequestered in his and her own solitude with nothing at hand to penetrate interpersonal barriers but an alienating medium of dissemblances.

Whitman insists, however, that this is not the case. Some may say "one word is as good as another, if the designation be understood" (*Pr*, 31), but actually, he asserts, each unique word belongs on natural principles to its designation. The easy substitution of signs does not prove language's arbitrariness. Rather, it manifests a decay in usage and a forgetting of those natural principles. Those who suppress the pronunciation, the genesis, and the employment of words in repartee and slang turn language into a pallid mechanism devised for the exchange of ideas. Their emphasis on words being "understood" affirms the priority of the cognitive function of words over their poetic value; any word will do so long as a meaning can be transmitted through it.

But words, according to Whitman, are not merely provisional carriers of severed abstract concepts. They grow, die, hurt, love, mourn, rejoice along with their human counterparts, for "when the time comes for them to represent any thing or any state of things, the words will surely follow" (*Pr*, 21). It is the poet's calling to make words act and feel again, to revivify those words that have been blunted and deadened by intellectual practices, filed away as "spectres in books" ("Song of Myself," l. 35) by scholars, linguists, and philosophers. If Whitman answers his own call and provides America with a living idiom countervailing abstraction and effeteness, his revivification will prove infectious and "the Americans [will] be the most fluent and melodious people in the world" (*Pr*, 2). With Whitman as its catalyst, America will achieve a vernacular poetic eminence that will corroborate its superior society and people. Because "the Americans of all nations . . . have probably the fullest poetical nature" (*PW*, II, 434), it only remains for "an American bard at last!" (*In Re*, 13) to draw it out and abet a stagnating culture.

Whitman's comments on the operative role words play in the manifest poetic destiny he postulates in *An American Primer* complete his exalted description of language's natural powers. By glorifying the organic, democratic roots of his medium and outlining his concomitant politico-poetic mission, Whitman both sanctions his own vocation and obviates the unnatural, alienating consequences of a theory of the sign based upon convention. Even though, in Whitman's theory, words are distanced from and a "result" of an original feeling, the line of descent is straight and true in a language, now existing only in America, innocent of intellectual or literary corruption. Because the sign is motivated, mediation acts not as a veil but as a pathway. In Europe, that pathway has become a thicket clogged with musty institutions, jaded beliefs, and outworn languages, but America still holds out the promise of a pure, natural language open to the directions of unadulterated emotion. With his impassioned sincerity and "one or two indicative words for the future" ("Poets to Come"), the vatic bard will guide his trusting readers tenderly to the final celebration of humanity in which integral soul and American "En Masse" are reconciled without compromise. America, that is, will be the glorious outcome of an old metaphysical history, the sublation of Europe and the West.

Language, then, whether facilitating the free individual expression of emotion or igniting an American teleology, plays a serviceable part in reifying a New World myth. By proffering a natural language ready for inspired usage, the American idiom assures the return of Orphic poetry. Like Orpheus, whose lyrics made rocks dance and heroes weep, animating all things in an ecstatic surrender to Pan, the American bard will exercise a prelapsarian language to reestablish man's primal bond with nature. To lead us back to what Emerson, in *Nature*, called "an original relation to the universe," the Orphic poet, whose ventriloquized and quoted words conclude Emerson's essay, will elicit from words their latent energies and, with the resistless authority that charmed the gods and reversed the laws of fate, undo the social repression of words' natural vigor. Through his expressive rhapsodies, the American Orpheus— "Walt Whitman, an American, one of the roughs, a kosmos"—will overcome civilizing tendencies that domesticate and inhibit emotion and draw his own Eurydice, nature, out of her culturally imposed exile.

Of course, Orphic poetry is impossible to achieve if one has only a tradition-laden, conventionalized language at one's disposal. (This is why Orphic poetry, like its "object," Eurydice, is never seen or heard directly, except as loss.) Whitman foresees how convention in language would nullify his project from the start, and so, in *An American Primer*, he naturalizes the sign to bolster his ambitions and ground his poetic undertaking. But notwithstanding its sweeping aggrandizement of language, *An American Primer* nevertheless contains passing references to the inadequacy or fallibility of words. Strangely enough, among the laudatory prophecies, Whitman sprinkles discordant observations betraying a skepticism regarding the natural powers of words.

Whitman not only laments the deficiency of words in expressing what lies within: "I feel a hundred realities, clearly determined in me, that words are not yet formed to represent" (*Pr*, 21); he also implies that words hinder the healthy exchange of feeling: "[The muscular classes of men] never give words to their most ardent friendships" (21), he says approvingly. At another point, he declares the significance of what remains unspoken, what resists verbalization: "What is not said is just as important as what is said and holds just as much meaning" (21). The dearth of words to express varied subjective experiences, the dampening of emotions when they are put into words, and the emphasis on the silence that words cannot touch—all three complaints parallel numerous other depreciative statements about language scattered across the corpus. They contribute to a critical motif running through Whitman's theoretical writings that is altogether contrary to and, curiously enough, side by side, his worshipful attitude toward language.

Whitman denigrates language for precisely the same reason he glorifies language: anxiety over its arbitrariness, the word's unreliability, its infidelity to nature. Though the strategies differ, the goals are the same—to rescue poetry from "impotence and dandyism" and restore it to its Orphic province and to expose the dissembling practices of specious writers and speakers. Arbitrariness founds and encourages these degenerate practices, for only a perversion of language's natural propriety could allow such abuses to occur. The natural language Whitman envisions is candid and clean, innocent and vital and passionate; it is the language of *Leaves of Grass*. To verify the natural character of *Leaves of Grass* and to provoke an organicist interpretation of his language and intentions, Whitman surrounds his poetry with prose remarks, many of which I have been re-marking and analyzing, that either affirm the natural basis of words or disavow their mediating function. To every edition of *Leaves of Grass* Whitman attaches prefaces, reviews, letters, notes, and so on, both his own and his critics', to clarify his conception of poetry and affirm that his poems are either natural or transparent. (He does not realize that the critical prose he hopes will prepare his readers to experience the poetry properly itself acts as a mediation.) In both cases, the purpose is to counter unnatural linguistic operations. Whereas in the former, Whitman abrogates arbitrariness by affirming a symbolic or a natural language, in the latter, he expresses a desire to dispense with language entirely. In other words, instead of focusing an attack upon literary or intellectual abuses of language, Whitman assails language on the basis of its inherent properties.

We can see Whitman, in conversation with Traubel in the spring of 1890, categorically expand his critique beyond the context of this or that particular usage and indict, as he says, "language itself *as* language," in order to hold out some ideal of poetic transparency: "I have always been best pleased with what seem most to disregard literariness: the artistic, the formal, the traditional aesthetic, the savor of mere words, jingles, sound—I have always eschewed: language itself *as* language, I have discounted—would have rejected it altogether but that it serves the purpose of *vehicle*, is a necessity—our mode of communication. But my aim has been, to subordinate that, no one could know it existed—as in fine plate glass one sees the objects beyond and does not realize the glass between" (*WWC*, VI, 386).

What begins as a specific dismissal of "literariness" quickly broadens into a wholesale condemnation of language itself—of, as he indiscriminately terms it, "our mode of communication." To repudiate "the traditional aesthetic" is a commonplace gesture made by literary figures in Whitman's time, just as noting such gestures is typical in much American Renaissance scholarship. But conceiving language abstractly as a "necessary *vehicle*" would seem to transcend historical conflicts between antithetical traditions, between past and present, Europe and America. The attempt to "subordinate" language implies that Whitman's anxiety is directed not only to influence but also to the medium itself, including the vernacular he previously extolled.

Whitman's anxiety over language per se forces him to confront, while failing to resolve, the contradiction created by his own metaphors: how can language be both "vehicle," an active instrument indispensable to communication, and "glass," a passive channel innocuously allowing a content to pass through it? It may seem that, because an instrument technically alters the raw material to which it is applied, language as "vehicle" is to be discarded, and that Whitman advocates polishing the "glass" to infinite clarity (at best, another oxymoron). But even a clear channel filters and frames a content passing through it according to its own structural properties. As Whitman says, there is no getting rid of language—it "is a necessity"—and however "fine" the "glass" is, it remains "between."

In other words, what Whitman wishes to be a distinction between contraries—"vehicle," technique, artifice versus "glass," ingenuousness, diaphanousness—is actually a relative scale of opacity. If one does not wish to give up this opposition and the entire taxonomy of poetic language founded upon it (organic versus mechanical, Romantic versus Neoclassical, Homer versus Virgil, and so on), the critical question then becomes, Which metaphors are the least catachrestic, the least damaging to the emotive origin in its maiden capacity? That is, Which metaphors are the least metaphorical?

If Whitman successfully answers the question of metaphorical degree, if he can make the medium into a "fine plate glass" whose relative transparency renders it negligible, then "no one could know it existed." Like the unheard music of the spheres, though it permeated our lives, language would remain unobtrusive and allow man a sense of nearness to others and to things. Man would live with the delusion that words can serve their provisional, transportational function and evaporate. Those wrong-headed aesthetes who enjoy "the savor of mere words, jingles, sound," he argues, would be subdued, for how could a poetry of "mere words" compete with a poetry of supralinguistic feelings? How could a poetry obsessed with technique, with a conscious, deliberate selection and revision and evaluation of words on the page, possess any emotional force, especially when compared with the spontaneous outbursts of the Whitmanian bard? In the pursuit of craftsmanship and refinement and agreement with acknowledged standards, putting "proper words in proper places," poets compromise their inspiration and produce, in Helen Price's paraphrase of Whitman, "mere verbal smartness."[11] But in disregard of "the artistic, the beautiful, the literary . . . the merely aesthetic" (PW,

11. Cited in Bucke, *Walt Whitman*, 30.

II, 770), Whitman will, like a "noiseless patient spider," spin poetry out of his own profound unconscious depths without bothering to reconcile his deepest emotions with such a superficial conveyance as language.

An implicit fraudulence may lie in this formulation, because we know how calculating and artful the poet's artless primitivism was, but Whitman's conception of poetry nevertheless accurately reflects how his contemporary admirers experienced his poems, or at least how they described that experience. Apart from the hyperbolic championing of the great man, the common thread running through Bucke's, O'Connor's, Burroughs', Kennedy's, and others' writings is an unremittent and uninterrogated emphasis on *Leaves of Grass's* natural emotive strength, the intense personal feeling immanent in Whitman's words but appreciable only by those whose human sensitivity and untutored apprehension of truth has remained unspoiled. Their refusal to interrogate repeats Whitman's almost to the letter (further evidence of Whitman's role in his defenders' compositions).

Though *Leaves of Grass* appears to be made of words, not emotions, and though Whitman painstakingly revised his poems both during and after the original inspiration with a ruthless critical eye, still, as previously noted, the Whitmanians reinforced the bardic myth of spontaneous utterance again and again in their commentaries. For example, Burroughs calls *Leaves of Grass* "a large, impassioned utterance upon all the main problems of life and of nationality. It is primitive, like the early literature of a race or people, in that its spirit and purpose are essentially religious. It is like the primitive literatures also in its prophetic cry and in its bardic simplicity and homeliness."[12] Setting aside the question of whether Whitman actually fulfilled his critical prescriptions, we can see how his votaries' responses provided ample evidence of his words' success in bringing about an emotional experience that transcended and abolished words. Some responses were so ardent that Whitman, in fear and dismay, politely discouraged any closer contact (for example, Anne Gilchrist, whose perusal of *Leaves of Grass* led to an obsessive idolatry of the poet that culminated in her desire to bear his children, a desire he could hardly have even considered satisfying). He found less dangerous examples of ecstatic emotional experiences that transcended language in his own life—experiences that, in fact, helped shape and clarify his poetics.

12. Burroughs, *Walt Whitman: A Study*, 73.

One moment of mute rapture unencumbered by words occurred when Whitman, while visiting Boston in the spring of 1860 to see his third edition of *Leaves of Grass* through the presses, attended numerous sermons delivered by Father Edward Thompson Taylor. This was the same seaside preacher who served as the model for Melville's Father Mapple in *Moby-Dick*. (Father Mapple was the ex-harpooner who counseled his "beloved shipmates" in the lessons of Jonah.) Twenty-seven years later, Whitman remembered the penetrating, tearful impression the aged orator made upon him. Whitman's short article in the *Century Magazine* notes Taylor's "grip," his "potent charm" and "volcanic passion." What made him so effective was that "when Father Taylor preached or prayed, the rhetoric and art, the mere words, (which usually play such a big part) seem'd altogether to disappear, and the *live feeling* advanced upon you and seiz'd you with a power before unknown" (*PW*, II, 550–51; the italics are Whitman's). Planted in the midst of Taylor's congregation, Whitman did not simply listen to his words for their meaning nor did he cautiously evaluate his sermon by orthodox principles. In his remembrance, Whitman ignores Taylor's ideas and avoids any discussion of Taylor's particular brand of faith.

Instead, Whitman records how enthralled he was with Taylor's "power before unknown," with the impact of his "*live feeling*," a dynamism no form or decorum or orthodoxy could capture and exhaust. By relegating language to its proper vehicular function so that the "mere words" would "disappear" upon reception, Taylor enables his "*live feeling*" to persist through its deliberate artistic rendering in words without deteriorating. Hence, Taylor's talent for arresting the souls of his listeners. Through Taylor's oratory, Whitman realizes how feeling and language can be sublimely reconciled, how a rhetoric that remained true to personal feeling was possible, though rare.

Taylor remained for Whitman a model of discourse (Whitman refers to him briefly but gratefully several times)—a humble, common sailor who put to shame the majority of speakers and writers in America. Whereas Taylor's language effaced itself in order to allow feeling to emanate through it, their "rhetoric and art" "play such a big part" in their discourses that feeling is virtually destroyed. As Whitman conceives the terms, "rhetoric and art" involve a conscious, technical subordination of genuine emotion to traditional social and literary codes, but "*live feeling*" rejects any such manipulation that might compromise its vitality. This is precisely, Whitman felt, what Emerson wanted him to do when, as they strolled along Boston Common during the same visit in 1860, Emerson advised Whitman to expurgate the *Enfans d'Adam* section of *Leaves of Grass*, presumably because of its sexual explicitness. (See *PW*, I, 281–82, for Whitman's account, written two decades later, of their meeting; Whitman's version makes no note of his rather ambiguous reception in Boston.)

Whitman acknowledged the validity of Emerson's objections, but deferentially declined acting upon them. In spite of Emerson's "argument-statement," "I felt," Whitman says, "down in my soul the clear and unmistakable conviction to disobey all and pursue my own way" (a thoroughly Emersonian response; *PW*, I, 281–82). To accede to social pressures would cause Whitman to betray the integrity of his soul, to manipulate and devalue an honest feeling in order to satisfy a repressive cultural interdiction. (Of course, in writing these unconvincing portrayals of heterosexual love, Whitman was enforcing upon himself a cultural interdiction.) The tools of that repression are "the mere words" that, because they do not necessarily coincide with the original impulse, may both deceive others and frustrate the healthy expression of that impulse. But whereas words generate hypocrisy and abet repression, *"live feeling,"* instinctive and guileless, abandons all disguise and pretense. As the unmediated presentation of an inner truth, feeling vigorously extends itself to others, and its peremptory "grip" will neither mislead nor corrupt; its salubrious verity is "unmistakable."

Whitman's encounter with Father Taylor was not the only time he felt the influence of *"live feeling"* penetrate his soul. Whitman also remembered Elias Hicks, the radical Quaker preacher, in the same terms, even though the fledgling poet was only ten years old when his parents took him to hear Hicks speak. In an extensive set of notes containing a few quotations from Hicks's own journal and some observations on Hicks's life and character, Whitman describes his impressions of that meeting in Brooklyn a half-century earlier and praises the doctrinal principles that Hicks advocated and were still controversial in 1888, the year *November Boughs,* in which the Hicks piece first appears, is published. In analyzing the effect Hicks had on an audience, Whitman again emphasizes the non-linguistic "unnameable something" underlying Hicks's speech that binds speaker to listener in a mutual emotional transport. Whitman writes: "If there is, as doubtless there is, an unnameable something behind oratory, a fund within or atmosphere without, deeper than art, deeper even than proof, that unnameable constitutional something Elias Hicks emanated from his very heart to the hearts of his audience, or carried with him, or probed into, and shook and arous'd in them—a sympathetic germ, probably rapport, lurking in every human eligibility, which no book, no rule, no statement has given or can give inherent knowledge, intuition— not even the best put forth, but launch'd out only by powerful human magnetism" (PW, II, 643). Whatever that "constitutional something" may be—Whitman believes we all feel it to a greater or lesser degree, but we can never know it rationally—it is certain that "no book, no rule, no statement" can adequately communicate it from one soul to another. It is "powerful human magnetism," not words, that furnishes the most effective transmission of the "fund within," the emotive force "emanated," "launched out" in electrifying streams, by an orator of Hicks's or Taylor's mettle. One could add to the list Emerson, Henry Ward Beecher, who met Whitman in 1856, several opera singers and stage performers, and Lincoln, who did not have the voice of the others but who certainly had the "magnetism."

In Whitman's somewhat imprecise phrasing (imprecise because of the elusive nature of the subject matter), "magnetism" instills "intuition." The former is a term Whitman lifts from popular pseudoscientific jargon and uses metaphorically to characterize the compelling attraction of certain men and women.[13] The latter is a term denoting self-evident, prelinguistic knowledge exempt from verification or falsification, immune to distortion, invulnerable to subversion because it simply is. This unspoken "is-ness" of "magnetism" and "intuition" springs from, as Whitman reported to Traubel, his profound "conviction that the thing is because it is, being what it is because it must be just that—as a tree is a tree, a river a river, the sky the sky. A curious affinity exists right there between me and the Quakers, who always say this is so or so because of some inner justifying fact—because it could not be otherwise. I remember a beautiful old Quakeress saying to me once: 'Walt—I feel thee is right—I could not tell why but I feel thee is right!'—and that seemed to be more significant than much that passes for reason in the world" (WWC, II, 143). Such "inner justifying facts" cannot be disputed, for

13. For Whitman's interest in animal magnetism, see Edmund Reiss, "Whitman's Debt to Animal Magnetism," PMLA, LXXVIII (1963), 80–88; and Harold Aspiz, Walt Whitman and the Body Beautiful (Urbana, 1980), 150–60.

they are not a product of "reason" or discourse, but rather are grounded in an ontic truth, a subjective "affinity" transcending individuals. As a result, one that provides the surest testimony to the lingering innocence of man and the superiority of democracy, speaker and audience are irrefutably bound in a shared ecstasy for which every human is "eligible," united in brotherhood by the equalizing "constitutional something" residing within everyone. Magnetism is the "adhesion," to use another of Whitman's favorite terms, drawing mankind together in a charged, energetic communion of souls. As opposed to words, magnetism, being a natural animating quintessence, retains some of the qualities of the soul whose impulses it delivers to other souls. Therefore, loosely speaking, magnetism is not exactly a mediation, at least not in the way words are.

By their supplementary action, words impede healthy contact between one's emotive core and another's. Craving a medium of expression that would act as a natural extension of itself, the soul can only regard words as alienating exterior signs perverting its self-present existence and causing the self loneliness and despair. Words draw the unique experiences of an individual soul into a familiar exposition recognizable more as a customary rhetoric than a singular expression of self. According to Whitman, the soul desires a return to the time before history, the mythical age of species childhood when all men could say what they felt candidly. Although the sounds of feeling precede the advent of culture, words always already belong to the order of history and discourse. They are learned, practiced, memorized; and so Whitman and Hicks will have as little as possible to do with words and their creations: institutions, discourse, prescriptions. For, in contrast with the pedant, "The eloquent man is natural": "His manner, his tones, his style, his argumentation, his feeling, his flight of fancy are all spontaneous results of his mind being fully occupied with his subject" (*NUPM*, VI, 2240).

Unlike the animal magnetists and mesmerists of Whitman's own time, who mastered a technical procedure and made a spectacle of hypnosis, Hicks employs his magnetism without "books" or "rules." He speaks directly "from his very heart to the hearts of his audience," all the while disdaining the ordinary preestablished conventions of oratory that can be mechanically reiterated to produce a desired effect. He creates a silent "rapport" that dispenses with the usual but superfluous courtesies and mannerisms, and reveals a "deeper" but forgotten congeniality among humankind. He appeals to the "sympathetic germ . . . lurking in every human eligibility," waiting to be cultivated by the irresistible presence of an inspired orator.

Whitman names this "germ" the *"inner light"* a paragraph later, but he minimizes any specific doctrinal principles the term might imply. Although Whitman does mention some articles of Hicks's creed, doctrine, in fact, contributes little to Hicks's formidable bearing: "It is mainly for the scene itself, and Elias' *personnel,* that I recall the incident" (*PW,* II, 644; Whitman's italics). Magnetism dwells in the individual, in the *"personnel"* qualities of the man or woman, not in his or her adherence to a belief. As Whitman says in an early notebook fragment (1854?), "The test of the goodness or truth of anything is the soul itself—whatever does good to the soul, soothes, refreshes, cheers, inspirits, consoles, &c&—that is so, easy enough" (*NUPM,* I, 187).

Yet, because Taylor and Hicks *were* sermonizers, because their magnetism apparently did bear some relation to the spoken word, it would seem that magnetism is not as supralinguistic as Whitman suggests, that the "mere words" do play more than a negligible role in facilitating intense emotional experience. We must remember that only through hearing the speakers' words does Whitman begin to sense the emotive truth underlying the words. Whitman himself acknowledges this; but in so doing he only begs the question of whether speech, in its highest form, and magnetism are one and the same or whether speech is simply the purest medium of magnetism, itself a medium of the unrepresentable.

Typically, Whitman leads his readers into ambivalences, for besides the assertions of language's relatively inconsequential function in communal emotional events, one can find several statements in Whitman's articles and notes on oratory and his favorite "voices" that establish a necessary organic connection between magnetism and speech.

That irresistible attraction and robust living treat of the vocalization . . . (*NUPM,* I, 407)

The amazing, splendid athletic magnetism of its vocalization. (*NUPM,* VI, 2224)

An irresistible latent vocal power and affect. (*NUPM,* VI, 2225)

The organs of the body attuned to the exertions of the mind, through the kindred organs of the hearers, instantaneously, and as it were, with an electrical spirit vibrate those energies from soul to soul. Not withstanding the diversity of minds in such a multitude, by the lightning of eloquence, they are melted into one mass, the whole assembly actuated in one and the same way, become, as it were, but one man and have but one voice. (*NUPM*, VI, 2239) [14]

"Vocalization" and "eloquence" possess "attraction," "magnetism," "power," and "electrical spirit," that particular emotional pull Whitman luxuriated in and hoped to exercise upon others in his own projected lecture career and through his poetry.

But does this imply that words are "energies"? Not in any ordinary sense of "words," for magnetism certainly does not carry any concepts or signifieds in its vital flow. What Whitman means by the term "vocalization" is not the articulation of words whose semantic import strikes the intellect but instead the utterance of sounds whose pitch and tone pierce the soul. Although the particular virtue that manifested Hicks's and Taylor's and any ideal orator's emotive magnetism was their electrifying voice, their oracular powers, as Whitman describes them, lay not so much in the meaning of the speaker's words as in the mere sound of those words. When witnessing great public speaking, Whitman responded acutely to its impassioned tones and lyric cadences (themselves resistant to abstraction or explanation), but he seems to have cared little for its content.

Indeed, here and elsewhere, although praising the sensory, phonic side of language, Whitman almost holds the intelligible, conceptual side of language in contempt. True to his deep-rooted anti-intellectualism and Jacksonian political bent, Whitman views abstract meaning as a pernicious ally, on a linguistic level, of rationality and logic. In celebrating "vocalization," an antilanguage, Whitman disposes of the signified and releases sound from the determinations of meaning, sensation from the confines of reason, so that the soul may experience freely and immediately the true presence of another soul. But, as we will see later, once Whitman has to confront the full sense of the word as sign as well as

14. Grier groups most of Whitman's notes and fragments on oratory in *NUPM*, VI, 2221–44. The first chapter of C. Carroll Hollis' *Language and Style in "Leaves of Grass"* (Baton Rouge, 1983) provides a thorough discussion of Whitman's lecture hopes. William L. Finkel's "Walt Whitman's Manuscript Notes on Oratory," *American Literature*, XXII (1950), 308–31, reveals that some of Whitman's writings are taken from contemporary textbooks on rhetoric. The last-quoted passage Finkel locates in Thomas Sheridan, *Lectures on the Art of Reading* (2 vols.; London, 1775).

force, the fact that the word is constituted as such by having a meaning, his enthusiasm for voice will find itself sharply marked and in question, and his poetics radically modified.

Whitman valued intimate contact with a vocal presence as one of the most significant of human experiences, for he reiterates his definition of "vocalization" (as sound divorced from meaning) and his high regard for it often, usually in his autobiographical writings. Whitman felt the magnetic charm of the "voice" influence him not only while listening to Hicks and Taylor preach, but also while attending opera and plays in New York in the 1840s and 1850s.[15] Along with the two orators, Whitman lists, in a late article (1890), the opera singers Marietta Alboni and Alle-sandro Bettini and the thespians Junius Brutus Booth and Fanny Kemble as examples of "the Perfect Human Voice." In the same note, he says, "Beyond all other power and beauty, there is something in the quality and power of the right voice (*timbre*, the schools call it) that touches the soul, the abysms" (*PW*, II, 674). That is, concepts and ideas appeal to the mind, but "quality and power," "*timbre*" (a purely sonic category), "touches the soul"—this is the measure of perfection. Likewise, when remembering Alboni in a brief draft of an earlier article (1858), Whitman again emphasizes sound over meaning: "Probably sweeter tones never issued from human lips. The mere sound of that voice was pleasure enough" (*NUPM*, I, 396).

That Whitman understood little of the language in which Alboni sang only enhanced his pleasure. (Italian opera reigned in New York during Whitman's years there as editor and critic, and in "Proud Music of the Storm" Whitman calls Italian opera his favorite.) Not knowing Italian, he could revel in the "mere sound" without interpreting it. By ignoring the abstract content, Whitman enables himself simply to delight in the words' sensuality, knowing that instead of being burdened with determining a conceptual meaning for the song, he can passively allow his own emotive energies to harmonize with the energy emitted by a perfect human voice. In disregard of intellectual protocols and critical evaluations, soul and voice consummate their natural affinity in an exquisite union that leaves him inspirited and shameless. Even though, after his

15. For the influence of opera on Whitman, see F. O. Matthiessen, *American Renaissance: Art and Expression in the Age of Emerson and Whitman* (New York, 1941), 558–63; Robert D. Faner, *Walt Whitman and Opera* (Philadelphia, 1951); and Floyd Stovall, *The Foreground of "Leaves of Grass"* (Charlottesville, Va., 1974), 77–100.

momentary abandonment, Whitman sometimes retreats into his oft-remarked "furtiveness," the experience of ecstasy survives in his memories as an ideal event in which social barriers to genuine human contact were, for once, stricken down.

Whitman has a similar reaction to a foreign language when Traubel's father reads German poetry to him. Whitman interprets his response the same way he interprets his response to Italian opera, interpretations that try to render a preinterpretive experience. He says to Traubel, Jr., "[Your father] was here the other day—sat over where you are sitting now—spouted German poetry to me—Goethe, Schiller, Heine, Lessing. I couldn't understand a word but I could understand everything else. . . . I was never so struck with the conviction that if everything else is present you do not need words. There he was, spouting away in a language strange to me—yet much of it seemed plain as if it was English" (*WWC*, I, 217).

Whitman sought to recreate such events in his poetry. When he insists that *Leaves of Grass* is not "mere literature" (see, for example, *Cor*, I, 348), when he claims the poem has a "physiological" effect on its attentive readers (see, for example, *NUPM*, IV, 1546, or *PW*, II, 468), or when he speaks of the *Leaves* in the same "electric" terms in which he describes "vocalization" (see his anonymous self-reviews in *In Re*), Whitman is arguing that the inspiring magnetic vocal presence to be felt in great oratory and song is to be felt in his own "songs" as well. That presence, we have seen, rests upon an exclusion and occulting of the signified and a privileging of the sonic. Put simply, pure sound coming from the heart is neither arbitrary nor artificial nor conventional. There is no essential difference between the medium and its origin. With the conceptual side of language bracketed, disguise, pretense, "aestheticism," and all hypocritical practices made possible by the sign's arbitrary dualism are obviated, and a healthy, natural truth prevails in human interaction.

But *Leaves of Grass* is not an oration. Its style and syntax may duplicate some of the typical rhetorical patterns of oratory, but it contains no physical gestures or vocal modulation, the very things Whitman concerned himself with most in his manuscript notes on oratory (see *NUPM*, VI, 2221–44). How, then, is Whitman to sustain the vocal-soulful presence in his poetry—a written, meaningful, signifying literary text? Whitman saw and heard Hicks, Alboni, and the like perform, but his readers have nothing to experience but silent letters that refer beyond themselves—cryptic, remnant hieroglyphs that suggest a lost presence, not an aural plenitude. Apart from continually denying his poetry's "meaningfulness" and "literariness," how can Whitman make the poetry itself undo its signifying action and replicate the unmediated energy of sound?

One possible answer may be indicated in Whitman's philological writings, where he occasionally toys with the possibility of a phonetic writing. In his notebook on words (*DN*, III, 664–727), Whitman inserts a clipping containing a "Specimen of Phonetic Printing" (709), he remarks on how journalists use a "phonographic shorthand" (710) to give precise verbatim quotations in their articles, and he cites dozens of phonetic transcriptions of uncommon or imported words. The point, of course, is to certify a word's proper spelling and pronunciation—"Pronunciation is the stamina of language" (*Pr*, 12)—so that their relation is as mimetic as possible. If orthography conveys pronunciation accurately, then writing will represent voice faithfully, and the reader, though removed from the vocal presence, will be able to reconstruct it.

Another excursion into phonetic poetics appears in a notebook entry (dated late 1860s) wherein Whitman speculates on writing a poem in which "each verse shall comprise *a call*" (*NUPM*, IV, 1385). He considers sounds such as the quail whistling "Phoo! Phoo! Phooet!" and children calling to cows with "Kush! Kush! Kush!" and horses with "Ku-juk! Ku-juk! Ku-juk!" and then he asks what are the "peculiar calls" characterizing different occupations. (One wonders why Whitman inserts an unnecessary diacritical mark in the middle of "Ku-juk!" when he is trying to strip writing of all nonphonetic elements.) The "call" appeals to Whitman because it is a natural sound designed to attract others by its repetitive, almost incantatory charm. Closer to the (non-)language of animals than to the language of men, the "call" testifies to a natural motive: animals "call" to satisfy hunger and love, to express fear and anger, to answer a natural need. Whereas most poetry, by translating those calls of nature into bookish, unrealistic terms ("Nobody ever talks as books and plays talk," *Pr*, 6), only frustrates natural desires, a poetic symphony of "calls" would give desires their most satisfying expression.

Whitman never actually wrote a poem of "calls," nor did he ever use a phonetic script. Instead, he wrote and revised *Leaves of Grass*. Whether he realized the impossibility of putting vocal presence into writing or whether he found the *Leaves* sufficient as it was to enable its readers to reconstruct its original "vocalization," Whitman's thoughts on phonetics never went beyond speculation and never became formalized into a poetic practice. *Leaves of Grass* does contain explicit praise for voice, and its stylistic patterns (simple present and imperative verb tenses, anaphora, apostrophes, rhetorical questions, catalogs, slang, and so on) mimic the rhetorical devices common to nineteenth-century oratory. But a mimicry of "vocalization" is not quite the same as the real thing, for in the translation from sound to writing, the vocal presence, the immediacy of the speaker's soul, is left behind. A silence ensues, a voiceless vacuum undercutting any unqualified judgment of *Leaves of Grass* as an oracular performance; but neither can it be judged as a failed oration, for that would imply that Whitman uncritically believed such a performance in writing was entirely possible.

To an extent, however, Whitman recognized the futility of striving to obtain an oral presence in his poetry (he understood his nostalgias better than he is usually given credit for). This is precisely why, in his attempt to discover a set of signs that would function as a natural manifestation of the soul, he struggled not only with aural signs but with a different order of signs as well. Specifically, Whitman also turned his attention to the way in which mute facial or bodily expression signifies the emotive truth lurking within. That is to say, in Whitman's poetry and prose, one can find, along with the privileging of voice, a fervent, opposite privileging of silent "physiognomy." To Whitman, physiognomy (or "Pathognomy," "countenance," the "face," the "look," all terms relating to the same phenomenon) is an even more immediate expression of or transparent window to the soul.

In one of his many lists of words intended for a dictionary, Whitman cites a definition of "Pathognomy" (like many of his entries, probably copied out of Webster, 1828 edition[16]) that clarifies his conception of bodily signs: "Pathognomy—the expression of the passions—the science of the signs by which the state of the passions is indicated—the natural language or operation of the mind, as indicated by the soft and mobile parts of the body" (*DN*, III, 815). Like phrenology, the pseudoscience in which Whitman held a lifelong interest, "Pathognomy" presupposes the existence of a "natural language" of the flesh.[17] The muscles,

16. Noah Webster, *An American Dictionary of the English Language* (New York, 1828).

17. For Whitman's interest in phrenology, see Stovall, *The Foreground of "Leaves of Grass,"* 154–59; and Aspiz, *Walt Whitman and the Body Beautiful,* 113–24.

the limbs, the countenance, the sexual organs, and so on, react to inner motivations or responses—"passions," not ideas—without premeditation, before social dictates intervene and channel passions into conventional forms such as language. A matter of neither custom nor arbitrary agreement, neither humanly devised nor understood as part of a praxis or discourse, "physiognomy" (the subject of "pathognomic" study) is beyond morals and culture. It is an integral part as well as a sign of the natural course of life. The carnal expression *is* the life.

In a healthy individual, one who has withstood institutionalization, exterior bodily signs follow instantaneously the soul's tameless vicissitudes, and so the close correspondence of physical appearance and spiritual-emotional reality is secure. Speech, in some cases, may represent the soul in the same concordant way that "physiognomy" does (that is, when speech becomes emotive sound), but because speech lacks a solid physiological basis, it always remains vulnerable to corrupting influences. Only an iconoclastic, charismatic speaker like Elias Hicks can resist the seductions of hackneyed traditional styles and use words strictly as a candid medium of honest feeling. Nevertheless, however provisional and self-effacing words may be in the mouth of an inspired orator, they still determine the phonic characteristics of the "vocalization" even though their semantic content has been shorn away. Even when praising Hick's "natural tone," Whitman slips in a brief footnote that undercuts voice: "The true Christian religion, (such was the teaching of Elias Hicks,) consists neither in rites or Bibles or sermons or Sundays—but in noiseless secret ecstasy and unremitted aspiration" (*PW*, II, 638). Therefore, "noiseless" "physiognomy," which lies nearest the soul and comes into being with it, is more trustworthy than the purest human speech, which still depends, to some extent, on a conventional language antedating the soul. "Physiognomy" is adequation, and it is, strangely enough, literally figural.

So, how is Whitman to work antiverbal physiognomy into his poetry? We can see the high value Whitman placed on physiognomic interaction from his descriptions of profoundly expressive faces he encountered personally, particularly Lincoln's, and from his disciples' reports (often written or edited by the poet) on how Whitman's own sublime countenance had a mysterious effect upon others. Whitman may be "eloquent enough of eye, posture, & expression" (*Cor*, I, 348), but how is Whitman to reproduce such physiognomic events using the printed page? He often asserts straight out the connection between poetry and physiognomy: "Literature means . . . the expression, of the body and contents and especially the idiocracy & spirit of a nation—and is its physiognomy" (*NUPM*, IV, 1601); "In the best poems appears the human body" (*NUPM*, I, 233); "Love . . . and your very flesh shall be a great poem, and have the richest fluency, not only in its words, but in the silent lines of its lips and face, and between the lashes of your eyes, and in every motion and joint of your body" (*PW*, II, 440–41). But he neglects to explain how the connection between poetry and physiognomy is established, how one generates the other. The famous portrait adorning the frontispiece of the 1855 edition exemplified exactly the type of *imago* Whitman wishes to present to his readers, but portraiture is not poetry.

Whitman does, in fact, attempt to create a portrait poetry in the early to middle 1850s when he writes a poem consisting of episodic descriptions of various local and historical scenes, complete with detailed "physiognomic" portrayals of assorted personages (including Emerson) and which he entitles "Pictures." Its rambling, populous content and oracular, free-verse poetic style mark this manuscript as the earliest evidence of Whitman's turn away from the decorous, sentimental verse he wrote in the 1840s. Although he never published the poem, the fragment contains many noteworthy passages, especially the portraits of Socrates and Christ, and Whitman did cull several lines from it over the years and insert them into his printed poems. But to bring the pictorial descriptions to life, to make the reader transcend the print and visualize the images in all their physiognomic expressiveness, Whitman must find a way to negate the words used to represent the images. Because physiognomy gains force from its mute character, its complete disregard for words spoken or written, Whitman must prevent his own words from depleting physiognomy's affective power. He realizes that "After all there is in eloquence and rage, / I guess there is more still in silence" (*NUPM*, I, 475); and so, in planning a poem, he counsels himself, "silence silence silence laconic taciturn" (*NUPM*, I, 234).

The point is that without the words to lead them, Whitman's readers will have to seek out his face and body for guidance, to scan his eyes and mouth and hands for self-evident signs of feeling. Whitman's physiognomy lies behind the poetry, awaiting our transcendent gaze. The poem itself functions as a momentary marker directing readers toward Whitman's peremptory countenance, historically one of the most photographed faces of the century. To reach that mute and serene poem of the flesh, Whitman's readers must obey the written poem's self-effacing "indicative words" that suppress their supplementary action and refer unmistakably beyond themselves. Confident that he possesses "that charm . . . which goes with the mere face and body magnetism of some men and women and makes everybody love them" (*DN*, III, 777), Whitman assures his readers of the sanitive effects of passing through and beyond the instrumental verse and settling upon his effusive flesh: "Touch me, touch the palm of your hand to my body as I pass, / Be not afraid of my body" ("As Adam Early in the Morning").

So, once his readers make actual contact with Whitman's corpus (his body and its surrogate, his book of poems), the mediating sign proves to be trivial and unnecessary, a superfluous cultural artifact obsolete now that the poet has vivified a natural, palpable poetry. When Whitman's physiognomy presents itself in the streets, on the ferries, in the photographs, and in the poems once the words have fulfilled their pictographic function, communication should achieve an immediacy that ordinary literary situations can never equal. Strictly speaking, physiognomy still involves signs, but physiognomic signs are neither culturally instituted nor are they foreign to their origin. Clearly, they are "less" cultural (granting that culture and mediation can be relative measurements) than speech or writing—or so Whitman would have it. Because, the poet assumes, physiognomic semiosis happens spontaneously and unconsciously, the sign itself emanates rather than represents the truth within. Hence, physiognomic signs need not be read; one should respond to them with the same unconscious, inarticulate spontaneity that originated it. Then will the mutual integrity and innocence of souls remain intact and pure "live" feeling endure.

This is the end of Whitman's poetics—a healthy, natural, unencumbered exchange of feeling. But such a simple formulation is belied by the practical and theoretical impediments Whitman encounters when attempting to write a poetry founded upon heartfelt emotive communication. He realizes that the pathway to immaculate expression is rarely trod and is choked by social contrivances severed from human emotion. To overcome social barriers and clear his own path, Whitman mounts an attack upon society's most ubiquitous and subversive fabrication—the artificial sign. To expurgate the artificial sign from human relations, Whitman both favors semiotic media that emanate naturally from the soul, and denigrates conventional signs that provide only tired, overused words—quotations—for the soul to reiterate in disclosing itself.

In sum, he recalls how "book-words" left him dispassionate and how certain voices and faces emboldened him. But, regardless of personal experience, the fact remains that Whitman cannot write poetry using natural signs. He may refer to real or imagined events where voice or physiognomy captured his soul, but he cannot use aural or pictographic signs in his poems. Constrained by a language bounded by convention, prone to decay, yielding to interpretation, Whitman nevertheless desires to circumvent it—a seemingly inescapable predicament.

The dilemma was unresolvable. But happily, it was the condition of a problematics that could be exploited and thus turned into a productive crisis. In his poems, Whitman brilliantly dramatizes his struggle with language, his attempt to find a natural idiom adequate to the soul. Then, he asks the reader to engage in a reverse struggle; that is, to decipher the soul that is using the language to represent itself. Whitman acknowledges the failure of written poetry to manifest or to present unmediatingly a pure feeling, but he develops that failure into a fruitful conflict, one involving himself and his writing and his readers and their reading.

Asking himself and his readers to surmount the poetic conflict by transcending the written words and encroaching upon the creative soul in its emotive purity, he turns his poetry into writing demands and reading requests. Not one to abandon his readers or to mystify them without reason, Whitman coerces, cajoles, and commands them to regard *Leaves of Grass* as a remedial juncture at which the way to human contact is begun. Whitman conducts his readers toward either vocal magnetism or physiognomic expression, signs that bear a closer relation to the soul than do written letters. In the proximity of voice or face, the final destination and origin, the soul, is in sight or within earshot. As a necessary prelude to the concourse of souls, the poem is essential. But to fulfill its properly provisional role in the return to natural signs, the poem must obliterate its own artificial characteristics, that is, its characters. The written verse must dissipate so that readers may pass through it and join the communal circle where, hearkening to the unifying presence of the bard, all heed his fervid Orphic voice and contemplate with wonder his revelatory countenance.

Whitman desires his poetry to work in this self-effacing way, to function as a theological discourse negating its own forms and setting the scene for innocent, natural communion. His ideal vision is so appealing that it is not hard to sympathize with Whitman's optimism and respond to his poetry accordingly. As we have seen, his many avid devotees, often surpassing the poet himself in zealousness, interpreted *Leaves of Grass* along "natural guidelines." In commenting upon the poems, they frequently resorted to musical or personal-physiological descriptive terms and tended to leave the actual language behind. Given contemporary formalist and theoretical methodologies, with their scrupulous attentiveness to language, one could treat Whitman's nineteenth-century admirers as naïve and uncritical, as idolatrous polemicists interested more in unleashing vitriol at repressive morality and traditional aesthetics than with focusing a careful eye upon the poetic language. No doubt there is a bit of truth in this. Anne Gilchrist's, much of O'Connor's, and some of Bucke's writings reveal more about the critics' values and desires and frustrations than they do about *Leaves of Grass*.

But the work of Burroughs, Kennedy, Symonds, Harned, Traubel, and many others rises above panegyric and often achieves a sensitive understanding of the poetry. Although these writers, too, concentrate on analyzing the spiritual qualities of *Leaves* and neglect its stylistic elements, this is due to their philosophical presuppositions, not to their shortcomings as critics. The assumption that leads Whitman's votaries to slight language derives from their refusal to question his argument for the unproblematic transparency of the sign (as it appears in *Leaves of Grass*) and their tendency to look him directly in the face, as it were. As pure and innocent as the language Adam used to name the animals, Whitman's language, in their view, excludes cultural accretions that blur access to the soul and includes only those words and phrases that allow Whitman's values and desires and frustrations to shine through without distortion. Because Whitman's language is a limpid, natural facade of the soul, it need not be analyzed or paraphrased or interpreted. As Traubel says in the introduction to *In Re Walt Whitman*, "Why violate the integrity of his own work with that of another, be this other however excellent?" (vii).

Today, scholars take a more critical attitude toward their subject. For those living in the wake of the "linguistic turn," the possibility of a transparent language is not simply doubtful, but unthinkable. One could easily point out the contradictions and fallacies in Whitman's poetics by invoking one of several convincing arguments against transparency (for example, Derrida's logic of the supplement, de Man's deconstruction of the Romantic symbol, or Austin's category of the performative), but that would not explain how Whitman's struggle with the sign, his attempt to naturalize it, informs his poems.

The following chapters try to do just that, to explicate the poems in light of the theoretical problematic I have outlined here. I contend that Whitman knew well the contradictions his theory led him into, but he clung to it nevertheless and welcomed those contradictions as the material of great poetry. Whitman's resulting dilemmas, prevarications, denials, and affirmations, all related to his ambivalent attitude toward the sign, are what makes *Leaves of Grass* the singular voluminous poetic event that it is. Whether one regards it as a comic "mixture of Yankee transcendentalism and New York rowdyism" (Charles Eliot Norton's phrase), a "most extraordinary piece of wit and wisdom" and a "remarkable mixture of the *Bhagvatgeta* and the *New York Herald*" (Emerson), or, in perhaps the most telling phrase Whitman ever uttered about his lifework, "only a language experiment," *Leaves of Grass* did, in ways Whitman could not anticipate, what it set out to do.

2

Composition

When Whitman published *Leaves of Grass* in July, 1855, he placed "Song of Myself" (as yet untitled) at the head of the dozen poems making up the first edition, and it has occupied a central position in Whitman scholarship and criticism ever since.[1] But Whitman never thought of "Song of Myself" or any other of his poems as presiding over or holding the key to the rest of the *Leaves*. Not wishing to view *Leaves of Grass* as a compilation of discrete units of verse, each with its own beginning, middle, and end, Whitman always speaks of his volume as an organic whole—"My poems, when complete, should be *A Unity*" (*NUPM*, I, 352)—and rarely refers to an individual poem by name. To Whitman, the *Leaves* constitute a "multeity in unity" synthesized by a profound natural necessity transcending any mechanical organization. They are a living aggregate evolving over time through successive edi-

1. For politically oriented readings of "Song of Myself," see Matthiessen, *American Renaissance*, 535–49; Richard Chase, *Walt Whitman Reconsidered* (New York, 1955), 57–98; Thomas, *The Lunar Light of Whitman's Poetry*, 40–71; Erkkila, *Whitman the Poetical Poet*, 95–117; and Kerry C. Larson, *Whitman's Drama of Consensus* (Chicago, 1988), 93–105, 114–28, 131–45. In Larson's emphasis on the problematics of "consensus" and the "tyrannies of 'Speech'" (p. 120), his reading anticipates my own.

For psychological readings, see Edwin Haviland Miller, *Walt Whitman's Poetry: A Psychological Journey* (New York, 1968), 85–114; Stephan Black, *Whitman's Journeys into Chaos: A Psychoanalytic Study of the Creative Process* (Princeton, 1975); David Cavitch, *My Soul and I: The Inner Life of Walt Whitman* (Boston, 1985), 45–71. For biographical approaches, see Gay Wilson Allen, *The Solitary Singer: A Critical Biography of Walt Whitman* (Chicago, 1955), 157–64; and Paul Zweig, *Walt Whitman: The Making of the Poet* (New York, 1985), 248–62.

tions as its two subjects, the poet and his country, evolved during the nineteenth century. Design and execution are simultaneous, and each separate utterance in the yet to be finished volume, like each individual citizen in America, though a unique expression of feeling, takes its contributory place in the ongoing process of the whole.

Multifarious in tone and content if not in style, filled with poems that end with little resolution or closure, matching the diversity of life with its own episodic parade of scenes and characters, *Leaves of Grass*, nevertheless, Whitman claims, is a complete harmonious gathering of spontaneous natural utterances whose cumulative significance exceeds the sum of its parts. What consolidates disparities and contradictions between and within individual poems, he says, is his fundamental intention in creating *Leaves of Grass*, what he loosely calls "the one deep purpose . . . the religious purpose" (*PW*, II, 461). Sometimes he gives this purpose an archival slant. In a letter to O'Connor, dated January 6, 1865, he praises *Drum-Taps* "because it delivers my ambition of the task that has haunted me, namely, to express in a poem . . . the pending action of this *Time & Land we swim in*" (*Cor*, I, 246). At other times, he declares a more egotistical goal: " 'Leaves of Grass' indeed (I cannot too often reiterate) has mainly been the outcropping of my own emotional and other personal nature—an attempt from first to last, to put a *Person*, a human being (myself, in the latter half of the Nineteenth Century,) freely, fully, and truly on record" (*PW*, II, 731).

Such announcements about the essential animus of his poetry are common in Whitman's articles, letters, and conversations, and they usually name either America or "Walt Whitman" as the main poetic subject. For Whitman to "record" a psyche or a society in all its seeming heterogeneity and accidence (though he believes certain universal truths lie hidden in the chaos of life), he must compose a book possessing a correspondent heterogeneity and accidence wherein each individual poem represents some partial aspect of America or of the self. Therefore, only when situated in the larger context of the completed book does a single utterance fulfill its purposive role in Whitman's grand design. But plucked from their natural environment, say, for reasons of expurgation to suit the moral demands of New England and British readers, particular poems no longer function in dialectical tension with other poems, and the book loses its coherence and integrity. (See *Cor*, III, 267, 270–71, 273, for Whitman's brushes with censorship.)

To maintain the balance and harmony of the whole and to infuse in the reader a proper respect for it, Whitman employs several editorial strategies, none of which, interestingly enough, substantially alter the poems themselves. He avoids using titles and section numbers in the first editions, he exercises scrupulous care in arranging the "clusters" in later editions, he oversees their printing, and he continues to resist (sometimes unsuccessfully) any abridgment. Also, by encouraging the division of readers into friendly and hostile "camps," ghostwriting much criticism of his poetry, and setting interpretive guidelines, he tries to preempt any future criticism that might despoil the sanctity of his life's work and analyze it to death.

But despite Whitman's prohibition of overly trenchant criticism and his insistence upon the organic unity of *Leaves of Grass*, critics have singled out "Song of Myself" as the best example of Whitman's literary technique and world view and also as the poem deciding the accuracy of the critics' own respective contentions. But "Song of Myself" is pivotal not only because it is the poem upon which depends the success or failure of critics' theories, but also because it is the one poem that remains the crucial testing ground of *Whitman's* poetic theory. Whereas the theoretical prose seeks to expel the arbitrary, conventional sign from poetic discourse, "Song of Myself," more often than any other poem in the canon, urgently and consistently manifests the desire to compel a spontaneous language of feeling, an idiom of sense and sensation as one. Coming after (in the first edition) a daunting, lengthy preface proclaiming America's need of a new style of poetry and a new race of poets, "Song of Myself" explicitly posits itself as just that—the exploratory, unfolding fulfillment, quickened by an inspired American bard, of a cultural prophecy (de Tocqueville's and Emerson's as well as Whitman's).

As such, it is a poem about writing and composition, about finding a language adequate to a certain emotional-spiritual import, in Whitman's deliberately vague phrase, "an interior not always seen" (*In Re,* 31). But it is just this self-conscious effort toward the unself-conscious that marks the problematics of Whitman's theory and generates the *aporias* (we might say, between statement and act) that, far from paralyzing his verse, initiates it and makes it expansive.

"Song of Myself" dramatizes the poet's attempt to found a transparent medium sympathetically adjusted to human pathos, and out of that staging come the poem's singular contradictions and ambivalences that have plagued critics and teased casual readers for over a century. These include the tentative search for trustworthy, candid signs, the cocksure dismissal of conventional, opaque "ornaments," and the frequent ironic parabases addressed variously to the readers or to himself, but always referring to reading or writing. They also include his speculations on the "meaning" of nature and of himself and the many "clews," "hints," "hieroglyphics," and other enigmatic signs scattered throughout "Song of Myself" that undermine the very transparency Whitman pursues. Whitman's master plot is the story of emplotment, the techniques and procedures and strategies of writing, and of how his natural composition will, he affirms, unleash evolutionary energies heretofore unfelt. In articulating in verse his ambitions and frustrations regarding language, Whitman draws his prime motivation—the quest for natural signs—*into the poem*, weaves it into the narrative fabric, confident that once he realizes a natural language in his poetry, man's restless insatiability will be appeased though never satisfied entirely—for the sign, natural or otherwise, is the very condition of desire, a situation Whitman was acutely conscious of. Thus sensitive, enlightened readers' innate powers, rejuvenated by having a compassionate language at their disposal, will be restored in their consanguine innocence.

"Song of Myself," however, is not the final achievement answering to Whitman's politico-linguistic hopes. Instead, it marks the critical path toward a resolution of those hopes, for Whitman spends less time affirming his success in recovering a redemptive natural language than he does negotiating with the obstacles hindering the anticipated recovery. Among those obstacles are an unimaginative reading public, a moralistic, conformity-minded culture, and, most of all, a lifeless poetic discourse. The resulting conflict—poet-protagonist versus his intractable antagonist, an alien language incompatible with human feeling—sends "Song of Myself" through experimental representations of different orders of signs (speech, writing, music, gesture, physiognomy) so that the initial desire for truth and clarity may end up in triumph. By incorporating its own theory, its own genesis and end, "Song of Myself" is an inherently "modernist" work, a self-reflexive poem relentlessly challenging the possibilities of its creation and openly presaging its incompletion.

Whitman inscribes the theoretical problematic shadowing him at his writing desk repeatedly in "Song of Myself," but the most sustained and far-reaching instance is Section 25. In this passage, Whitman juxtaposes several brief dialogical pronouncements involving familiar but antagonistic partners whose verbal exchanges articulate the poet's fundamental obsession, the question of *writing* a natural language:[2]

> Dazzling and tremendous how quick the sunrise would kill me,
> If I could not now and always send sunrise out of me.
>
> We also ascend dazzling and tremendous as the sun,
> We found our own my soul in the calm and cool of the daybreak.
>
> My voice goes after what my eyes cannot reach,
> With the twirl of my tongue I encompass worlds and volumes of worlds.
>
> Speech is the twin of my vision....it is unequal to measure itself.
> It provokes me forever,
> It says sarcastically, Walt, you understand enough....why don't you let it
>   out then?
>
> Come now I will not be tantalized....you conceive too much of articulation.
>
> Do you not know how the buds beneath are folded?
> Waiting in gloom protected by frost,
> The dirt receding before my prophetical screams,
> I underlying causes to balance them at last,
> My knowledge my live parts....it keeping tally with the meaning of things,
> Happiness....which whoever hears me let him or her set out in search of
>   this day.
>
> My final merit I refuse you....I refuse putting from me the best I am.
>
> Encompass worlds but never try to encompass me,
> I crowd your noisiest talk by looking toward you.
>
> Writing and talk do not prove me,
> I carry the plenum of proof and every thing else in my face,
> With the hush of my lips I confound the topmost skeptic.
>
> (ll. 560–81)

This is a compressed, plurivocal, convoluted lyric, accelerating and decelerating with characteristic Whitmanian unpredictability. Indeed, at

---

2. The ellipses in the quotation that follows are Whitman's. Throughout this book, Whitman's ellipses are given as he gave them—with no intervening spaces between the ellipsis points. My own ellipses, on the other hand, do have intervening spaces, each of which is equal to a normal space between words—the standard practice in modern scholarly books.

first glance these lines would seem to bear little connection with one another and the entire section to have no common narrative or thematic thread. The different participants in these illusory speech acts—poet, nature (the "sunrise"), soul, voice, reader, "skeptic"—nimbly intermingle without any logical progression, making it difficult for the reader to follow the argument. Because Whitman often applies, here and elsewhere, personal pronouns to inhuman or inanimate objects and impersonal pronouns to subjective forces and impulses, it is hard to establish with certainty the references of "I," "you," "we," and "it," a problem testifying, for some critics, to the crudity of Whitman's art and the sloppiness of his idealism.

But this is to overlook the critical shift taking place here, for, rather than clumsily directing his cast of speakers in a formless debate, Whitman is actually inverting what has been the major thrust of his poetics. That is, as the words flow from voice to voice in the course of Section 25, Whitman is subtly enacting a diametric transformation in the status of his utterance so that what began as a shortcoming and a transgression of his basic principles—his recalcitrance in the face of nature's profuseness—ends as a virtue, the purest expression of natural feeling: the physiognomic silence that promises a "plenum of proof" too profound for words to render.

The passage begins with Whitman citing nature's challenge to him as a poet: "Dazzling and tremendous how quick the sunrise would kill me, / If I could not now and always send sunrise out of me." This is the imperative Whitman proposes to himself when he sits down to write—to respond to nature's beauty and energy with a reciprocal beauty and energy, to radiate from his own simmering emotive core the same sensuous power and splendor the sun radiates. But to mimic or, rather, participate in nature's meaningful workings without breaching any *natural law* (an oxymoron, but one Whitman would not quite have recognized as such), the bard must avoid either impoverishing nature by regulating its pristine energy with a stale poetic language or adding to nature by encumbering it with extravagant idiosyncratic tropes.

Rather than overspreading yet another superfluous layer of perfunctory signs upon nature's placid exterior, the poet must, to use a favorite term of Whitman's, "tally" nature, both in the passive sense of "be fitted to," "suit," or "correspond with" nature and in the active sense of "measure" or "balance" nature (see Webster). The poet must become "the channel of thoughts and things without increase or diminution" so that the poem may achieve "the art of art, the glory of expression and the sunshine of the light of letters . . . simplicity" (PW, II, 443–44). In other words, his art will return to artlessness, to a natural simplicity uncorrupted by technique, calculation, artifice.

In his projected natural poem, Whitman will rise above conventional practices yet curb any artificial excesses and then, he hopes, indeed "speak . . . with the perfect rectitude and insouciance of the movements of animals and the unimpeachableness of the sentiment of trees" (PW, II, 443–44). Put simply, as Whitman writes in his first Preface, "What I experience or portray shall go from my composition without a shred of my composition" (PW, II, 444–45). To repress any evidence of "composition," the remainder of which would indicate an *un*natural genesis, Whitman must dispose of the poem's technological components (the manufactured book, its print, spacing, pagination, and so on) and deny its historical development (the conditions under which he wrote, the revisions he made, the maturation of his style, his place in a literary tradition). For both of these imply an unnatural historical contingency; namely, a mechanical, deliberate, self-conscious strategy, as opposed to a spontaneous overflow of powerful feeling. Because, as Whitman says, "I will have nothing hang in the way, not the richest curtains" (PW, II, 444), nature will shine forth from the song with prelapsarian clarity and directness that shall awaken readers from their quotidian slumbers and draw them out of their stifling "houses and rooms" (l. 14) and into the "open air" (l. 1251), compelling them to slough off their cultural baggage—fashions, finances, intellectual and literary manners and idioms, class—and experience nature "undisguised and naked" (l. 19).

The opening couplet of Section 25, then, encapsulates the purpose of "Song of Myself"—to create another nature. But *another* nature cannot simply be conflated with something like nature itself. This second nature is not a golden world to lift us imaginatively out of this brazen world; Whitman's biodical vision denounced otherworldly philosophies because they depreciate this world by regarding nature as false appearance or as valueless, purposeless, amoral existence. And it is not a mere derivative and secondary "mirror of nature"; that would imply a mimetic theory of poetry, one that reduces creation to an impersonal copying procedure that would hardly suit Whitman's Orphic, expressive conception of the poet. Instead, Whitman intends to create a "Nature without check with original energy" (l. 13; this line and the seven lines preceding it do not appear until 1881), a "Nature" unburdened by convention.

But such a formulation merely begs the question of how this written "Nature" made new, although being neither a transparent window to nor a faithful copy of "actual" nature, is to possess "original energy." If nature is, in Nietzsche's relevant phrase, "a work of art that gives birth to itself," in what dilemma is the writer placed who wants at once to engender a *natural* art (an oxymoron) and in that act withdraw from his creation? If the shapes and meanings he fabricates are to correspond to those of "actual" nature, what about the poem's written character? How is the supplementary letter to be disposed of? In what way can its manufacturing be suppressed? Herein lies the poem's counterinspiration, the inscribed problematics that haunt the poet's desire for auto-insemination.

Should Whitman waver in his quest, nature is always there to reprimand him and guide his "composition" toward its proper outcome. "Song of Myself," as a tentative critique of writing, a preparatory analysis of its own creation, positions these critical reproofs enacted by nature's representative within the poem as part of its dialectical but unsystematic movements. Frequently, Whitman finds himself halted by a natural force or delegate that confronts him, as the sunrise does in Section 25, with his cardinal purpose and his errant pursuits (generally attributed to an abuse of language):

> The spotted hawk swoops by and accuses me....he complains of my gab and my loitering. (l. 1331)
> And the look of the bay mare shames silliness out of me. (l. 244)
> The press of my foot to the earth springs a hundred affections,
> They scorn the best I can do to relate them. (ll. 253–54)

The verbs "accuses," "shames," "scorn," and, earlier, "would kill," directed toward Whitman's "gab," his attempt "to relate" or "send sunrise out of me" (in other words, to write natural poetry), seem rather harsh and melodramatic to describe the actions of what is presumably a benevolent Being tendering health and security to those who heed her sublime ministrations. But nature is not only a meaningful, liberal presence offering freedom, truth, and value to each individual. She is also a "discipline" (Emerson), peremptory and unforgiving, especially for the poet who, intentionally or not, threatens to supplement nature with his own extrinsic, impertinent signs and meanings. In creating another nature, the poet elaborates upon what needs no elaboration, writes what cannot be written, signifies and differentiates what is and should remain pure and self-identical. He is always in danger of transgressing the inviolate truth he seeks to preserve. Although Whitman judges all institutional activities as greater or lesser crimes against nature, and believes his own Orphic poetry to exceed other social performances in restorative power, he still feels a constant "shame."

To dramatize his shame, Whitman has nature chastise him, as above; to expel his shame, he castigates the technical side of his art that mistreats inspiration and abuses nature:

You shall no longer take things at second or third hand....nor look through
    the eyes of the dead....nor feed on the spectres in books. (l. 35)
This is the breath of laws and songs and behaviour,
This is the tasteless water of souls....this is the true sustenance,
It is for the illiterate. (Deleted after 1871, these lines originally came after
    l. 360.)
Oxen that rattle the yoke or halt in the shade, what is that you express in
    your eyes?
It seems to me more than all the print I have read in my life. (ll. 235–36)

Instead of provoking a natural experience bringing communal understanding and proximity to nature, writing appeals only to the literate, those encased in their private studies, their attention focused on a dead past, their interpretations dividing natural, universal truth into solipsistic, idiosyncratic opinions. Although nature remains constant and simple yet abundant and unrestricted, writing relies on regulation by technics or propriety, which, as conventional, can change through history. It takes places after the fact, involving a separation from and an attempted reconstruction of the natural course of things. Writing is its own problem.

How, then, is Whitman to naturalize writing? How can he offset the arguments he himself levels against writing? He says that writing mechanically disrupts communion, that it segregates individuals into isolated, self-absorbed readers, and that it is subject to interpretation and history. Contrarily, he says that voice bespeaks and physiognomy manifests raw human experiences and shares them naturally. They occur only in the present and are bounded by an authoritative origin (speaker or "looker"), and therefore escape the novelties of interpretation and history. Besides refusing to use any artificial techniques or unnatural contrivances when composing (or at least claiming to do so), the only way for Whitman to naturalize writing so that his poetry will seem to follow an organic process is to invert his terms and then to interpret nature, including his soul, as a form of writing. If nature, like *Leaves of Grass*, is a "book" composed of natural signs, a theological text comprised of *natura naturata*, the sensuous language of nature, and *natura naturans*, its animating meaning (a dualism that satisfies Whitman's vaguely pantheist-Christian world view), then Whitman's vocation, though treated disdainfully from the perspective of a nontextual conception of nature, would prove innocent of breaching the natural order. Its semiotic gestures would replicate faithfully those nature performs.

Whitman occasionally follows precisely this strategy in "Song of Myself." At certain moments, he casts himself less as a writer spinning natural truths out of his galvanizing soul than as a reader who must decipher or "translate" nature or his soul (which appears to him as an enigmatic text) before passing it on to his audience, the secondary readers:

To me the converging objects of the universe perpetually flow,
All are written to me, and I must get what the writing means. (ll. 404–405)

I find letters from God dropped in the street, and every one is signed by God's name. (l. 1286)

I wish I could translate the hints about the dead young men and women. (l. 121)

I am the poet of the body,
And I am the poet of the soul.

The pleasures of heaven are with me, and the pains of hell are with me,
The first I grafted and increase upon myself....the latter I translate into a new tongue. (ll. 422–24 in the last edition)

And I swear I never will translate myself at all, only to him or her who privately stays with me in the open air. (l. 1251)

Merely reinscribing a natural code frees Whitman of the charge of textualizing a nontext. Whether that code contains the objective "writing" or "hints" or "letters" that mystify nature and arouse Whitman's curiosity, or the subjective "pleasures" or "pains" originating in the self that he then, respectively, "grafts and increases" or "translates," the literatus avoids doing violence to nature. That is, because nature is *not* an undifferentiated, monadic simplicity, *is* already fractured by the dualistic structure of representation, and, as such, is susceptible to misinterpretation and concealment of "what writing means," Whitman need not lament the textual, plurivocal character of *Leaves of Grass*. Instead of treating his poetic writings as mechanical perversions or complications of pure, simple nature, Whitman can regard those consequences as proper results certifying his text's fruitfulness.

Whitman solidifies the identification of his text with nature's text in Section 6, where a "child" asks him, "What is the grass?" The question refers at the same time to nature, to the volume's title, and to Whitman's writing. He responds with a series of suppositional tropes indicating the ubiquitousness of signs and the necessity of interpretation, whether one is in "the open air" or in the library: "I guess it must be the *flag* of my disposition, out of hopeful green stuff *woven*. / Or I guess it is the hand-kerchief of the Lord, / . . . / Bearing the owner's *name* someway in the corners, that we may see and *remark*, and say *Whose?* / . . . / Or I guess it is a uniform *hieroglyphic*, / And it *means*" (ll. 101–107; my italics, except for "*Whose?*").

Of course, this textualizing of nature reverses the usual thrust of Whitman's poetics—to naturalize the text. But how else is Whitman to escape or deny the gratuitous foundations of his activity, writing "this printed and bound book" (l. 1088)? By shifting back and forth between contradictory positions—nature as signifying text versus nature as self-present unity, poet as Orphic origin versus poet as subordinate translator, words as natural extensions of feeling versus words as enervating conventionalizations of feeling—and recording that unpredictable oscillation (the outcome being "Song of Myself"), Whitman mitigates the guilt of writing. In other words, by thematizing writing and all its condemnatory ramifications, by making writing the subject of writing and articulating its fall from or agreement with nature, Whitman appeases his anxiety over creating perhaps yet another body of collateral, arbitrary, supplementary signs.

We can see a parallel naturalization process take place when Whitman tries to free of sinfulness that other perversion of nature, often linked to writing, which he feels compelled to represent often in "Song of My-self"—masturbation. Like writing, masturbation operates through il-lusory, imaginary signs that displace the thing itself and render Whit-man guilty of self-abuse, of expending his natural energies upon abstract images and fantasies. Although he has less apparent anxiety over mas-turbation than he has over writing, many exultant autoerotic episodes are still accompanied by a sense of danger and ridicule or a fear of ex-posure (see, for example, the entirety of Sections 28 and 29). But to expel his guilt and check the severe judgments of ascetic moralists who preach upon the degradations the body seduces us into, Whitman says frankly: "I believe in the flesh and the appetites, / . . . / Divine am I inside and out, and I make holy whatever I touch or am touched from" (ll. 522–24).

Believing that what is natural cannot be sinful but only innocent and healthy, Whitman celebrates his self-directed ejaculations as a joyous hu-man acceptance of nature's vitality, impassioned and just responses to the sublime fertility that engendered the world. Man, however, has fallen away from such naturality. In Section 22, when he says to the sea and its "crooked inviting fingers," "Cushion me soft....rock me in billowy drowse, / Dash me with amorous wet....I can repay you" (ll. 452–53), Whitman promises to "repay" nature for giving him life and comfort with vigorous upsurgings of his own "amorous wet." He reiterates his obligation in Section 25, for the phrase "send sunrise out of me," which I interpret as "writing natural poetry," refers also to masturbation, espe-cially when reading in light of the couplet appearing five lines earlier: "Something I cannot see puts upward libidinous prongs, / Seas of bright juice suffuse heaven" (ll. 555–56). But both references—to writing and to masturbation—lead to the same conclusion: for Whitman to succeed as man and poet, his poetic genius–masculine potency must rival nature's fecund creativity; his self-propelled songs and semen must match the sunrises, ocean waves, animal calls, and other instances of nature's own narcissism.

Following the opening couplet in Section 25, which summarizes con-cisely the simple yet perhaps hopeless task Whitman burdens himself with, is another couplet that suggests that his fears have abruptly been allayed: "We also ascend dazzling and tremendous as the sun, / We found our own my soul in the calm and cool of the daybreak." The first "We," when carried over from the preceding lines, would seem to refer to the poet and his genitalia as Whitman enacts his male version of the dawn, but the second "We" denotes unambiguously Whitman and his "soul." Although inklings of a sexual satisfaction and womblike security underlie the latter image, the references to "soul" clearly spiritualizes the autoeroticism described earlier and shifts the context from that of a masturbatory fantasy to a quietistic, though still natural, meditation. The substitution of "calm and cool" for "dazzling and tremendous," along with the transition from the negative conditional "If I could not" to the assertive "We found our own," indicates that whereas Whitman is threatened by an outside nature, which images forth exempla of creativity the poet struggles to remain faithful to, Whitman is soothed by an inside "soul," which replenishes.

Whitman establishes this closeness in the beginning of the poem where he says, "I loafe and invite my soul, / I lean and loafe at my ease....observing a spear of summer grass" (ll. 4–5), and gives it metaphysical proportions in Section 5, where he recalls, "I mind how we lay in June, such a transparent summer morning" (l. 87). This is the passage that mystical critics from Richard Maurice Bucke and William James to James E. Miller, Jr., and Roger Asselineau have interpreted as a straightforward recounting of an actual mystical experience the poet underwent sometime in the early 1850s and strove undauntingly to represent adequately in "Song of Myself."

As Whitman and these critics would have it, when the poet is in intimate concourse with his soul, the desire for expression dissolves and the theoretical commandment that says "Be a natural sayer!" becomes intrusive, for Whitman's relationship with his soul is secretive, self-enclosed, and, generally, nonverbal. As "that unspeakable Something . . . which makes [Whitman] know without being able to tell how it is" (*NUPM*, I, 183), the soul eschews language and grants knowledge intuitively to those resolutely faithful to its sanctifying effects. But although it disdains language and its exteriorizing processes, preferring instead the sheltered, private enclosures of self-sufficient self-presence, the soul also acts as a transcendental, probational authority secured from the play of signs. The soul scrutinizes an utterance's sincerity and condemns anything at variance with its natural instincts: "The soul never once has been fool'd and never can be fool'd" (*PW*, II, 451); "Whatever satisfies the soul is truth" (*PW*, II, 748).

Though it promises a reassuring certitude stabilizing Whitman's beliefs and answering his appeals, the soul does not make judgments. Judgment requires discourse, logic, law, and interpretation, and hence institutes a conventional, mediating standard between Whitman and his soul, the very manifoldlike barrier Whitman wants to exclude from their relationship. In Kantian terms, judgment presides over the particular (in Whitman's case, a discrete natural emotion) by subsuming it under the universal, a rule, principle, or law, that which has been socially constructed and maintained by intellectual thinkers and legislators and critics. But like the "Me myself," the soul serenely disregards the "Trippers and askers" (l. 66) who use "mockings or arguments" (l. 81) to prove a point. With a conviction founded upon natural truth, not ratiocination, it unmistakably makes itself felt and affects Whitman pleasurably or painfully without using intermediaries. Although Whitman gives the soul a voice in Section 5, what it sounds is not articulate speech but a low, nirvanic "hum":

Loafe with me on the grass....loose the stop from your throat,
Not words, not music or rhyme I want....not custom or lecture, not even the
    best,
Only the lull I like, the hum of your valved voice.

(ll. 84–86)

The soul's "lull," a blank expression of power and truth, the aural by-product of cosmic energy *in potentia*, has no conceptual denotation. It makes up a natural language of humanity, consisting of a single, undifferentiated phoneme that simply says "happiness" (l. 1318). That "part" of human nature (a pneuma, not a faculty) capable of experiencing the boundless, uncensored joy Whitman foresees as the goal of "Song of Myself," the soul is the principle of universal attraction.

Believing that "any degree of development in the soul is only responded to by the similar degree in other souls" (*NUPM*, VI, 2055), Whitman must, like Hicks and Taylor, penetrate the gratuitous layers of cultural adjuncts suppressing the natural powers of other souls and obstructing their contact. To intensify his confidential allure and kindle languishing psyches, Whitman knows he must echo the soul's "valved voice" and vocalize his own "hum," and so he insinuates (without actually enunciating) an occult sound into his poem, a sound whose semantic import precedes ordinary categories of sense and whose aural magnetism

will bond Whitman and his readers in a sonic embrace, an "afflatus surging and surging" (l. 505):

> I chant a new chant of dilation or pride. (l. 428)
> And mine a word of the modern....a word en masse. (l. 478)
> I speak the password primeval. (l. 506)

These dynamic, mystical sounds unify souls in a communal rapture,
what conventional language has sundered. Archetypal and natural, they
clear a powerful incantatory pathway undeviatingly into the souls of individual listeners and raise them, "old and young" (l. 330), "maternal as
well as paternal" (l. 332), "the wicked just the same as the righteous"
(l. 373), into a community of visionaries whose voices are lifted together
in an impassioned "chant democratic."

But Whitman does not write down the "password primeval"; he does
not tell us what the "word en masse" is. He withholds the Logos and
to our anxious yearnings replies with Emersonian half-consolations:
"You are also asking me questions, and I hear you; / I answer that I
cannot answer....you must find out for yourself" (ll. 1223–24). But
Whitman's forbearance is due less to a philosophy of self-reliance than it
is to his recognizing the implications of inscribing the Logos. Although,
in vocalizing the communal meaning, Whitman's voice brings a universal
import to discrete utterance, his pen, in putting soul-inspired sound into
script, commits it to a nonphonetic conventional notation, and thus sets
the scene for discursive analysis. Worst of all, it perhaps alters its pronunciation, which *is* its "meaning" ("Pronunciation is the stamina of
language," *Pr*, 12). In other words, to write the Logos would destroy the
organic unity of sound and soul, opening up between origin and sign a
representational space that makes possible distortion and falsehood.

In intersubjective terms, writing divides souls into insulated corre-
spondents transmitting their feelings through the letter, souls that would
otherwise experience life sympathetically through their consonant at-
tunement to the universal call. Because sound properly inspires a non-
cognitive emotional reaction in the souls, not the intellects, of its listeners, interpretation does not come into play, for there is no play, no
room for variation. There is no distance between representation and represented, sound and its emotive "content" or motivation, that needs to be

crossed. Whitman acts out in fantasy this coexperiencing in Sections 33 to 37, where he describes in brutal detail various scenes of suffering (the shipwreck, the "hounded slave" and "mashed fireman," the Goliad massacre, the *Bonhomme Richard*) and then projects himself into messianic identifications: "I do not ask the wounded person how he feels....I myself become the wounded person" (l. 845); "all these I feel or am" (l. 834); and, in a measured and deliberate tricolon carrying the authority of actual lived experience, "I am the man....I suffered....I was there" (l. 832). Tying these scenes together and facilitating his martyrdom is Whitman's "own voice, orotund sweeping and final" (l. 1055): "My voice is the wife's voice" (l. 820); "All this I swallow" (l. 831); "I am the old artillerist, and tell" (l. 858); "Hear now the tale" (l. 875; later deleted).

Voice, then, democratic in its appeal and hypnotic in its attraction, is the primal medium conveying feeling from soul to soul. Residing in the private inner space of passions and desires and memories, yet retaining the power to change the world, voice protects the soul from being enveloped by the letter. Because the soul is always in danger of circumscription by signs that meagerly represent the "pent-up aching rivers" longing for release, Whitman privileges sounds that owe their existence to nothing outside the soul and welcomes only what is "our own," regarding anything not originating in the soul as superfluous exteriority. Although writing records the soul's emotive impulses and, hence, after they have departed, leaves a remainder, a perfunctory sign of their absence, sound, having no foundation other than the soul, is as transient as the passionate turns of the heart that generate it. In other words, writing stabilizes and spatializes a changing, temporal be-ing, a core of selfhood that "resist[s] anything better than [its] own diversity" (l. 1349). Writing consolidates desire or intention into a stasis, preservable and lifeless, severed from the identity that tired to replicate itself and create a form in its own imageless image.

But sound is as evanescent as the shifting essence it socializes: it vanishes as it is uttered, just as desires and thoughts vanish in a succession of sensations. Because spoken words or mystical sounds dissolve as they are realized, they can never cause self-estrangement, the alienation of the soul. Remaining proximate to feeling, and being just as ephemeral, sound appears indistinguishable from the soul it presents. By imposing script upon the soul's instinctual actions, writing retards the spontaneity of natural pronunciation. It robs expression of all the human accompaniments of heartfelt communication—gesture, tone, touch—leaving only the exiguous residue of black signs on white paper.

And so Whitman summons his readers to hearken to "the belch'd words of [his] voice" (l. 25), to appreciate his impulsive utterances as gushing forth from the natural wellsprings of his emotive ebbs and flows. Writing makes its appeal through dry-as-dust pages of forgotten books, but voice decisively grasps other souls in its alluring magnetism: "My voice goes after what my eyes cannot reach" (l. 564). Whitman's eyes remain confined to a linear world of images and print. As opposed to "voice," which spreads its captivating energy in all directions, the eye passively receives along a narrow perspective a phenomenal world of distant pictures. Whereas sound emanates from the soul and returns to (is heard by) the soul simultaneously, sight has no way of returning to its origin. The nearest sight can get to the soul, or the only way it can form a closed circle with the soul at the center, is by looking in the mirror, but what it sees there is merely a facade, another object in the world. This discovery of absence when gazing upon himself causes Whitman to question whether *he* is simply another object thrown into the world and whether the soul's creations are just more self-delusions.

But what do sight's skeptical implications ("the terrible doubt of appearances") amount to when compared with voice's confident mastery of the universe? Sight may remain caught in a shadowy realm of appearances, but voice penetrates to the heart of things, to the in-itself and the in-himself. With flamboyant ease and unswerving truthfulness—what is natural cannot lie!—voice boldly answers or renders moot all doubt-ridden questions and ends Whitman's ontological insecurity. After he decides, just after Section 25, that he "will do nothing for a long time but listen, / And accrue what I hear into myself" (ll. 582–83), it is "the sound of the human voice....a sound I love" (l. 585) that leads him to "the puzzle of puzzles, / And that we call Being" (ll. 609–10). His own voice is no less revelatory and comprehensive: "With the twirl of my tongue I encompass worlds and volumes of worlds" (l. 565).

That is, Whitman's voice takes in both "worlds" and books of philosophies of "worlds" (and, in a pun on "volume," the noise they produce). Voice oversees reality, be it an objective universe or a subjective *Lebenswelt*, and language, the factitious superstructure overlaying but not necessarily corresponding with reality. Voice "pronounces" nature's beauty and sublimity—"what my eyes cannot reach"—and incorporates society's goods and evils: "What blurt is it about virtue and about vice? / Evil propels me, and reform of evil propels me" (ll. 464–65; Whitman's all-inclusive, counterprivative attitude is his theodical way of overcoming evil and suffering in the world).

Also, like the "morning-glory at [his] window" which, in its innocent, delicate repose, "satisfies [him] more than the metaphysics of books" (l. 549), voice has the power to silence intellectual aspersions and to expose corrupt sophistries. Simply by living its spontaneous, natural existence, voice becomes the yardstick by which all other discourse is measured, including Whitman's own poetry. But though voice adjudicates, in a sense, all other creations, it does so unreflectively: "Speech is the twin of my vision....it is unequal to measure itself" (l. 566).

Like the "I" that "was never measured, and never will be measured" (l. 1201), voice, by its unpredictable, sublime, overreaching action, exceeds all calculation. It can never be parceled by any numerical rigidity, especially poetic meter. For speech "to measure itself" would imply a dualism within speech, a reflective distance from which it can evaluate or represent itself. But speech is unitary and univocal; it is not a product of self-consciousness. The "vision" of which speech is a "twin" refers not to the "eyes" noted earlier, but to the founding inspiration of poetry, the unformulated, un-"measured" impulse of creativity. As vision's "twin," Whitman's speech is born(e) with it in a natural awakening, before self-reflexivity and cultural standards and techniques have tamed his vision and classified it according to recognizable genres and forms. Because vision and speech come into being simultaneously, the doubling that takes place is not mimetic, for mimesis presupposes a primary ideal and a secondary copy. Only the relationship between this dual origin and its (their) written record is mimetic. Whatever does, in fact, mimic vision or voice, whatever reproduces them violates their private integrity, opens the perfect circle of self-sustaining self-presence to the language of a plundering other. It translates the soul's original outbursts into depleted quotations, causes its "howls [to be] restrained by decorum" (l. 164). For we must remember that inspiration itself can never, strictly speaking, be repeated. It arises without prescription and passes away under unique conditions, leaving only traces, signs of its departure.

And yet Whitman finds himself using a public language and slipping back into conventional rhetoric and literary tradition, despite his earnest fidelity to the emotive truth harbored within. That nourishing store of feeling nestled among the pulsations of his heart resists exteriorization and secludes itself inside the limit marked by the sign. But by maintaining that reserve, Whitman suffers the reproval of his Orphic impulse, the need for expression previously called "Speech": "It provokes me forever, / It says sarcastically, Walt, you understand enough....why don't you let it out then?" (ll. 567–68).

Rather than being the aural equivalent of his inspiration, "speech," vaguely distinguished from "voice," is now a sarcastic outside observer of the creative process, "provoking" him to fulfill his Orphic mission. Speech repeats the accusation that "the sun" implicitly leveled against him a few lines earlier: "Walt, you are failing to be a natural sayer. All around you and inside you lies a natural truth awaiting your lyrical pronouncements, and yet you loiter, prevaricate, lounge around, waste the day and squander nature's gifts and delay the sacred coming you yourself prophesied and aspired to." Claiming that his indolence is merely an intentional stance—the pose of "the magnificent idler"—designed to salvage men from their "lives of quiet desperation" (Thoreau) and the "mania of owning things" (l. 689) is not enough to justify withholding his deepest feelings from expression. Giving vent to his feeling takes precedence over social reform (the former is a necessary prerequisite of the latter) and, as "speech" indicates, Whitman "understands enough" to achieve what he has desired all along—heartfelt expression. So why does he refrain from doing so?

The answer lies in the fact that "speech," a critical listener of the natural utterance, must call Whitman's attention to the neglected inner "it" supposedly grounding his poetry. This inverts the usual relationship between the origin of inspiration and the secondary language that represents it. In examining the genesis Whitman proposes here, we see that, instead of having a pure, natural origin—one compelling him to shed his critical discourse and allow for a spontaneous expression—this "speech" is actually a critical language, a secondary utterance that, although denouncing criticism, postulates its own authority and then requires that Whitman remain faithful to it. Whitman gives a primary voice to the critical "outside" and, in so doing, puts into question all speech, critical and poetic, and subverts the logocentric genetic model he generally affirms. Regis Durand's intriguing but all too brief commentary on Section 25 neatly describes this basic reversal succinctly enough to merit repeating:

But what is being performed here? Nothing less than the invention of an inner self, of the self as a hoard of words, as a receptacle of unspoken words, as intimate and secret self: the invention of secrecy itself. The injunction to utter what the subject is supposed to know, to hold within himself, by making it possible *not* to say it, does in fact create the possibility for a secret. Speech may claim its due, insist that the subject "let it out" . . . but by doing so, it draws a line between what can be said and what cannot be said: it gives rise to the very idea of a secret, of the unspeakable.[3]

That is to say, the creative origin, here Whitman's prelinguistic core of feeling, actually is a "creation" of the language it ostensibly wields: in the beginning is the *word*, not the soul or psyche or "Me myself." The word constitutes "the unspeakable," delimits its perpetual absence, and declares itself shamefully inadequate to represent it fully and purely and innocently. Whitman does not "let it out" because he cannot "let it out." "It" must remain a "hermit in a poet's metaphors" (Stevens), an "inside" inaccessible to but necessitated by every "outside" that signifies it. We cannot call the "outside" the agent of this differentiation; for not only is the causality already structured by difference, but we cannot even "think" this irreducible differential structure without succumbing to it and being implicated in it. Each "letting out" only adds to the edifice of the reclusive "within." Despite Whitman's promises to the contrary, that he will "wash the gum from [reader's] eyes" and present them with "the dazzle of the light" (ll. 1229–30) of unmediated emotion, "it" ultimately escapes Whitman's expressive powers.

The metaphysical margin instituted by the very words Whitman wishes to use to recuperate what lies beyond it prevents him from articulating the cherished unspeakable "it." Failing to display it in his poems, he feels disconsolate over the relative ineffectiveness of even the most inspired poetic language. But even if language defers rather than

3. Regis Durand, "The Anxiety of Performance," *New Literary History*, XII (1980), 168.

effects the immediate expression of feelings, he can still find hope in language's *indirect* assurance of "its" existence. Though Whitman cannot
describe, predicate, image, characterize, or in any way signify "it," he can
still worship "it": "There is that in me....I do not know what it is....
but I know it is in me" (l. 1309):

I do not know it....it is without name....it is a word unsaid,
It is not in any dictionary or utterance or symbol.
Something it swings on more than the earth I swing on,
To it the creation is the friend whose embracing awakens me.
Perhaps I might tell more....Outlines! I plead for my brothers and sisters.
Do you see O my brothers and sisters?
It is not chaos or death....it is form and union and plan....it is eternal life....it
    is happiness.

(ll. 1312–18)

Even when he "might tell more," Whitman delivers only empty abstractions—"form and union and plan." The best he can give is "Out-
lines!" Although the bard is certain of the beneficence and grounding
authority of his emotive interior and can say with blank confidence, "I
know it is in me," a simple, irrefutable testimony to his direct awareness
of feeling, nothing more about "it" can be said. Because feeling resists
conceptualization and verbalization—"I do not know what it is"; "It is
without name"—Whitman must resort to definition by negation ("not,"
"without," "unsaid").

The last phrase in Section 50, "it is eternal life....it is happiness," by
virtue of the indubitable copula, sounds like a resolution or at least a
clarification of what "it" might be. But "eternal life" is an ambiguous
term in "Song of Myself." Is "eternal life" the immortality of the soul—
"And my spirit said No, we level that lift to pass and continue beyond"
(l. 1222)—or is it the passage of Whitman's decomposing flesh into other
life forms—"I bequeath myself to the dirt to grow from the grass I love, /
If you want me again look for me under your bootsoles" (ll. 1339–40)?
And how does the notion of "happiness" accord with the numerous detailed and bloody scenes of suffering portrayed in "Song of Myself" that
Whitman willingly projects himself into? Even the copula causes confu-

sion and raises the old problem of substance versus accident: are "happiness" and "it" one and the same, or is the former a consequence of or accompaniment to the latter?

The contradictions and ambiguities of Whitman's syntax and terminology—the rhetoric that at once asserts his desire for the transcendental essence and withholds its availability—force Whitman to reconsider momentarily the scope and intent of his poetic project. Whitman may accept those contradictions and flaunt them in his poetry as the poetic disseminations of a fecund sensibility, a "kosmos" expanding "afoot with [his] vision" (l. 716), but the actual reason for his prevarications he cannot abide. That is, Whitman must condemn the way language both appropriates and disguises feeling, arrogating what it can and imprisoning what it cannot. The feelings language does render become traditionalized, situated in a referential structure that has its own history. This structure assumes the status of a fallen exterior, a conventional system of languages and laws and customs and proprieties no longer guided by a natural origin, human feeling.

Language, then, masks pure feeling, provides only conventionalized, distorted, exiled versions of what at first arose naturally and spontaneously in the heart. Not even spontaneous utterance or organic symbolism can draw pure feeling out of its natural seclusion: "It is not in any dictionary or symbol." And so Whitman, to return to Section 25, relinquishes hope for a return to a preconventional idiom and quite simply rejects language, written and spoken: "Come now I will not be tantalized. . . . you conceive too much of articulation" (l. 569). Despite its dictatorial demands, "Speech," the "you" referred to, shall not lure him into a self-defeating practice. What speech "conceives too much of," both gives birth to and overvalues, is not natural expression but "articulation," the verbal tool of rationality and erudition.

"Speech" misapprehends its product, for articulation is an unnatural conception, a conceiving that breeds concepts, words, and ideas without substance. That is, articulation rarifies into abstraction the "living and buried speech . . . always vibrating here" (l. 164). Articulation sacrifices those unconscious vibrations of the heart, which we experience as euphony and rhythm, for intellectual clarity or polished urbanity. The sensuous language of the heart thus comes to fit systematic classifications, such as Kant's Categories, or to yield to the clever turn of phrase rather than touching the inner chords of intuitive truth. Whereas natural signs may not be substituted for, articulation rests upon or is simply another name for substitution. There is an instantaneous one-to-one correspondence between natural sign and emotive origin: smiles and laughter follow immediately from joy, tears and grimaces from pain. But one may articulate one's joy or pain in an infinite number of ways using different signs each time.

Opposing this proliferating articulation, which strays further and further from the thing itself, is not only natural expression, but also the purely nominal language lying relatively close to nature, the transparent sign system in which each word-noun stands unequivocally for thing. Whitman regards this noun language as the most primary and essential of all verbal constructs: "Language may have since been scraped and drenched down to the completer state, which makes the verbs the centers, for grammatical purposes; but, in the nature of things, nouns must have been the first, and remain essentially so" (*DN*, III, 715; dated 1856–1857). In an ideal language of names, words remain bound to a concrete, specific situation. Because they resist abstraction, they are endowed with the unique singularity of objects. There is no ambiguity, no distortion, no slippage in the word-thing relationship, for the sign always functions as a direct "pointing-toward" an object. Because there are, as yet, no statements or propositions or subject-predicate formulae, and hence no falsehoods (or truths), linguistic acts involve no interpretation. What little is added does not corrupt the straightforward perception of the world.

But articulation takes this simple, undeviating language of spoken gestures and complicates it, elaborates upon it. Articulation (*articulus*, "joint") draws connections and marks relations between things, adding prepositions and verbs and articles and modifiers to nouns, building intricate syntactical structures and compound verb tenses, making possible abstract hypothetical and conditional cases. In general, it turns attention to the description and away from the described. For Whitman, the net result is that the simple, present reality seen with his eyes and felt in his soul is entangled in a grammatical web, filtered through an opaque screen of markings to the extent that common human experience becomes not the certain intuition of clear and distinct presence, but the chancy interpretation of dubious representations. Consequently, as articulation disrupts an immediate awareness of what *is*, it can only be suffered as a displacement both of the things themselves and the soul.

What reversal has Whitman engineered here in his response to "speech"? At the beginning of Section 25, he feels threatened by nature's creative abundance, fearing that if *Leaves of Grass* does not match nature in beauty and energy and life, he will have failed to satisfy his own poetic credo and fundamental beliefs. Whitman responds by affirming the familiar proximity of his "soul," in whose company he easefully reclines in the "calm and cool of the daybreak." Out of their comradeship, "vision" and "voice" spontaneously burgeon forth, proclaiming their mastery over the universe and giving Whitman confidence in his bardic powers.

Yet voice's proclamation is not to be confused with Whitman's poem: in "Song of Myself," the poet too often retires into passivity and seclusion and "furtiveness" for his poem to qualify as a visionary impulsive utterance. He gives too much consideration to signs and to writing, he deliberates too self-consciously over his manner of presentation, and he suffers too much anxiety over the past (tradition) and the future (interpretation) to qualify unproblematically as the new American Orpheus. A few lines later, Whitman's hesitation sets him up for "speech's" accusation, "why don't you let it out then?" If Whitman has the capacity for expression, why does he meddle with signs and falter on the brink of song? Why does he not let the magnetism flow, why not unveil the emotive reality pressing for annunciation?

But although the question seems simple enough, in fact, "speech's" demand, by its critical nature, radically inverts Whitman's usual hierarchy of discourse. What should be original and unpremeditated and *inarticulate*—the bardic outcry of feeling—must actually be initiated and called for by a derivative, analytical, ironic language of criticism. That Whitman, at this point, is unable to produce an inspired utterance might indicate the poet's failure of feeling or his inability to obviate tradition and convention. But with the next line, "you [speech] conceive too much of articulation," Whitman shifts the blame from himself to his medium, the means with which he expresses and socializes and publicizes himself. It is not a defect of "Personality" or a lack of poetic talent that induces Whitman's furtiveness (in those cases, his covert pose would serve merely to rationalize or disguise his shortcomings as a natural poet). Rather, it is the camouflaging effects of language that force him into a position of secrecy.

That is, the unmediated emotion Whitman wishes to render in *Leaves of Grass* will not stay pure, undifferentiated, and self-present once words are attached to it. Therefore, despite attempts to represent it, pure feeling remains concealed, withheld from signification. Henceforth, feeling acquires the status of a mystified truth, a transcendental origin inaccessible to language (which comes to be seen as guiltily inadequate to its source), leaving Whitman with nothing to do but ruminate upon his abrupt, unsuccessful encounter with the Sublime. Thus Whitman reverses the critical judgment. Previously condemned as a token of his remiss delinquency, this stillness is now redeemed as the mute precondition of an alternative medium that transports feeling to others yet respects feeling's natural integrity. It is a set of signs that, having no independent properties, follows immediately the promptings of feeling—physiognomy.

Yet before turning to the "face," to what and how it "means," Whitman appeals to examples of nature's secrecy and withdrawal that, by analogy, justify his own:

> Do you not know how the buds beneath are folded?
> Waiting in gloom protected by frost,
> The dirt receding before my prophetical screams.
>
> (ll. 570–72)

That "gloom" and "frost" and "dirt" surround the "buds" and hinder their emergence does not in any way defile them or rob them of life. Like William Carlos Williams' sluggish roots and grasses struggling to take hold in the muddy fields ("By the road to the contagious hospital"), Whitman's "buds" possess a potential dignity and beauty and power that cold, darkness, and death, themselves integral parts of life, do not tarnish or cripple, but only postpone. The "buds" sit in "waiting" for Whitman's "prophetical screams," the inseminating natural Logos that clears the ground, making the "dirt recede" so that a new life may begin.

But those "screams," it should be noted, are not part of a language. They do not function within a conventional system of differential relations whereby they acquire meaning and value. Instead, they are "cries of nature" (Rousseau): inarticulate, physiologically based, instinctual responses to sensation, prerational, almost preconscious eruptions of passion, without meaning or reference, but with a certain forward-looking, effectual, "prophetical" energy. Like the "wild gander['s] . . . Ya-honk" which, though "The pert may suppose it meaningless," has "its purpose and place up there toward the November sky" (ll. 245–48), Whitman's "prophetical screams" have an unspoken, nonsematic import. They do not mean; they bring forth life.

Any further elaboration or explanation of the natural "cry" only denatures it, needlessly complicating its native simplicity. The "screams" must remain pure and free, carefully disentangled from critical extrapolation and appraisal. Having "loos'd [them] to the eddies of the wind" (l. 25), Whitman cannot provide didactic guidelines to help his listeners interpret his "screams," for that would imply either an intellectual closedmindedness in his audience (which interpretive assistance would merely add to, not penetrate) or the want or infirmity of his utterance. If his utterance does not take effect immediately, it will have failed, and no amount of repetition or analysis will make restitution for its neglect. Although, as he says, "My words itch at your ears till you understand them" (l. 1246), this "understanding" is not to be arrived at discursively, for this knowledge is supposedly proleptic, and therefore requires only inducement, not argument, for it to become clear. Ideally, Whitman will edify his listeners and his listeners will countenance Whitman in the same way that "the animals," "so placid and self-contained" (l. 684), prevail upon him and he receives them: "they show their relations to me and I accept them; / they bring me tokens of myself....they evince them plainly in their possession" (ll. 692–93).

Although signs ("relations," "tokens") mediate this poetic intercourse, Whitman can easily "accept them" because the animals "evince them plainly" and the signs they manifest symbolize in some manner his natural self. With a recognizable, comforting sympathy inhabiting their concourse, everything is preunderstood and interpretation is unnecessary. There is a mutual inner attraction, a symbiotic "procreant urge of the world" (l. 45) breeding "a knit of identity" (l. 47) prompting Whitman to seek in their nature some affinity certifying his health and inspiring his poetry:

> You sea! I resign myself to you also....I guess what you mean,
> I behold from the beach your crooked inviting fingers,
> I believe you refuse to go back without feeling of me;
> We must have a turn together.

> (ll. 448–51)

Although Whitman longs to make contact with "the sea" and goes so far as to "resign" himself to it, the sea comfortingly beckons him closer with its "crooked inviting fingers," its waves irregularly petering out on the sloping sand. By "feeling of [him]," the sea communicates the meaning (Whitman often connects it with his mother and/or death), which he can only guess at, try to intuit. Thus they "must have a turn together" so that their fellowship may be consummated. By maintaining contact with this silent tactile-emotional "feeling" of and with nature, by entering into poetic-erotic dalliances with the sea, the animals, the sun, and the woods, Whitman strengthens his poetic ambitions and vindicates his *in*articulation. The poet thus affirms once more his fitfulness, his instinctual correspondence with nature (Section 25):

I underlying causes to balance them at last,
My knowledge my live parts....it keeping tally with the meaning of things,
Happiness....which whoever hears me let him or her set out in search of this
    day.

                                                  (ll. 573–75)

The "I" is both ground and reflection, Orpheus and Echo. In "underlying causes to balance them at last," the "I" is the motivating source of action and the ultimate reconciler of conflict, the cause of causality and the arbitrator of contradiction. In "keeping tally with the meaning of things," the "I" is the consort of objective truth ("All truths wait in all things," l. 648), the recorder of the immanent "meaning" of natural phenomena. Through its Orphic mastery, the "I" regulates all natural effects, but it does so unobtrusively, remaining apart while observing nature's narcissistic pleasures. Out of this constant, unproblematic oscillation (not a dialectic) comes "Happiness," the enduring quiescent joy Whitman celebrates at the end of "Song of Myself." It grows out of "knowledge" and "live parts," intuition and genitalia, two spontaneously reactive and grasping facets of Whitman's "personality" "balanced" here in verse by paratactic juxtaposition.

By placing "Happiness" alone at the beginning of the line (as he isolates it at the end of Section 50 with the simple declarative, "it is happiness"), Whitman gives the word an occult status, implying that "Happiness" is more than just another feeling among many others. For "Happiness" is, to Whitman, the be-all and end-all of life, the origin and end of human activity, and thus the *name* of his poetic self. It reconciles body and soul, truth and error, good and evil, mortality and immortality, through its universal emotional existence. Its immanent *is*-ness dwells in everyone, putting to rest all ethical and metaphysical uncertainties before it irresistibly unites man and woman, master and slave, prostitute and spinster, into a utopian community. "Happiness" is the first inalienable right.

As such, as a natural, benevolent, indistinguishable presence that is simply there within all men and women, grounding our hopes and desires (though stifled by our cultural inventions), "Happiness" cannot be signified. It can neither be differentiated, analyzed, or even understood, for it is a suprarational totality felt, not known, by accommodating souls. "Happiness" refuses to be absented by any supplementary stand-in, by any order of signs whatsoever, and so Whitman has no way of communicating it. Although he cherishes "Happiness" as the highest good, he must, so to speak, keep it to himself—to adapt it to a medium so that it may be transmitted to others would be to despoil it. And besides, each person already has his or her own "Happiness." There is no need to communicate it, but only to inspire it. Whitman's voice can initiate but never satisfy one's longings: "Not I, not any one else can travel that road for you, / You must travel it for yourself" (ll. 1210–11).

Fortunately, this metaphysical block accords with Whitman's sociopolitical ideas of pedagogy and influence (*the* Emersonian dilemma). Simply to give "Happiness" to others would prove to be an act of power and imposition, one leading to all sorts of dependencies, abuses, and misinterpretations, thus preventing the reader from making on his own the kind of jubilant self-discovery the poet has made. True, Whitman makes occasional arrogant proclamations of dominance: "You can do nothing and be nothing but what I will infold you" (l. 1002); "In all people I see myself" (l. 401); "Magnifying and applying come I" (l. 1026). But these function more as catalysts instigating readers to become a "kosmos" and realize themselves than they do as edicts subjugating readers beneath Whitman's tyrannical egotism.

After having emancipated readers from their institutional shackles, Whitman would prefer that they "repay the same service to [him]" (l. 1218). Instead of trying to assemble a group of blind followers who would worship him before God and even before themselves, Whitman counsels his readers in the virtues of self-reliance (although, it should be noted, the former is exactly what Whitman tended toward in his later years):

> Long have you timidly waded, holding a plank by the shore,
> Now I will you to be a bold swimmer,
> To jump off in the midst of the sea, and rise again and nod to me and shout,
>   and laughingly dash your hair.
> I am the teacher of athletes,
> He that by me spreads a wider breast than my own proves the width of
>   my own,
> He most honors my style who learns under it to destroy the teacher.
>
>   (ll. 1231–36)

Because "the teacher's" verse style is a limpid extension (motivated by "happiness") of his soul that has cleared the way for a genuine revelatory expression as unique and original as its provenance, it cannot properly be repeated by anyone else. Each self naturally has its own particular "style."

To copy another's is to become a slave to custom, to oppress one's free creativity through an apish imitation of another's accomplished forms. Style should be organic, not mechanical—a continuous enlargement of self, not a separate mediation between self and other. Style should be a trait, an innate set of tendencies, not a sequence of habits or learned responses and mimicries. Each soul contains within itself its own singular principles of growth that need no cultivation or acculturation.

To safeguard individual development, to protect self-discovery from being overshadowed by doctrine and morality and learning, Whitman teaches a subversion of teaching, an abeyance of "creeds and schools" (although he does admit that "Book-knowledge is important as help to one's personal qualities," [NUPM, I, 323]). He ultimately disclaims the authority of priests, schoolmasters, politicians, and critics. Believing that "The boy I love, the same becomes a man not through derived power but in his own right" (l. 1237), Whitman tries to convince readers to ignore historical and institutional authorities and confront themselves. He writes: "The saints and sages in history....but you yourself? / Sermons

81

and creeds and theology....but the human brain, and what is called reason, and what is called love, and what is called life?" (ll. 1094–95).

In Whitman's case, the obstacles preventing him from coming into his own—in other words, becoming Walt Whitman, the American bard—and obtaining a concomitant original style lay in styles inadequate to the liberal exuberance of young America. A language whose rhetorical patterns are based upon a literary past slips too easily into an obsolete, impersonal style and traditionalizes the original self. But a language that, though rhetorical, would be a "new" rhetoric based upon the directions and idiosyncrasies of the desires of "a simple separate person" ("One's-Self I Sing," l. 1), would becomingly unfold the self and secure its unique identity. And now that, in "Song of Myself," Whitman has indeed achieved a pure language of the self, it only remains for readers, if they desire the "happiness" that comes with the natural celebration of one's soul, to do the same.

Yet their pathway must be different if they are to be true to their individuality, a fact Whitman realizes only too well from his struggle with Emerson's influence. (We can see evidence of Whitman's conflict from his famous admission to Trowbridge in 1860 that "I was simmering simmering simmering; Emerson brought me to a boil," and his later denial that he had even read Emerson before writing *Leaves of Grass*.[4]) This turnabout marks the operating contradiction that at once haunts and animates Whitman's rhetoric. The poet extends the critic's formulation by casting himself in the shadow not only of precursors but of revisionists "to come" as well. The reader's task is not to accept the content of Whitman's argument but to find his or her own autochthonous form, the one muscular style and syntax equal to each respective soul. Hence, Whitman's reserve: "My final merit I refuse you....I refuse putting from me the best I am" (l. 576). To give his "best" would inhibit the reader from discovering his and her "best." As we shall see, this hypothesis will become particularly troublesome to Whitman following the publication of the first edition, when he realizes that influence can work in both directions, that belated readers can exercise just as much power as original poets.

This political-stylistic reading, if carried to its conclusion, would perhaps serve to explicate sufficiently Whitman's poetics were it not for the fact that his critique of language is more radical than such a reading im-

4. Trowbridge, *My Own Story*, 367.

plies. As we have seen, Whitman's analysis is not focused upon this or that usage, but upon language or the sign itself, the transgressive tower of Babel that fractured Adam's inarticulate natural idiom into "so many uttering tongues!" (l. 119). Though it would seem that Whitman's strategy often starts from a political division of languages into original and fallen, natural and artificial, vernacular and "literary," American and European, and so on, in fact these pairs constitute not a value-ridden spectrum of languages but rather a polar opposition between language and nonlanguage. Whereas the latter languages are sign-systems composed of historically determined designations bound only by the tenuous law of convention and prone to abuse and manipulate Truth ("what *is*"), the former (non-)languages are neither composed nor invented nor historical, for they preexist convention. They are bound by the fixed, universal law of nature and are indissolubly tied to the Truth they mediate. Though the original natural language may involve signs, these signs came about through the initial act of signification, the first naming that took place at a time when nature still guided man's behavior, when sign making was a simple, straightforward process and the just-represented "meanings," which obsess Whitman so much, remained securely at hand. Natural signs, or "etymons," functioned as necessary, motivated expressions of the thing they signified, be it object or feeling. A natural sign's only significant relation was to its signification, a given, extratextual outside and not another sign. Hence, according to modern conceptions—language is a limitless play of differences—a natural language is not a language. It is a fixed set of discrete organic labels of real identities.

Whitman's decision to "refuse putting from me the best I am," then, is due more to the pitfalls of using a conventional language to signify himself than it is to a political resolve to avoid suppressing the reader. Whitman withholds his "final merit" because he wishes to maintain its purity, goodness, and health, to prevent it from being differentiated and parceled out by an alienating system of signs. As a "finality" putting an end to interpretation, Whitman's "merit" is not simply some message to be communicated, some content waiting to be formalized. It is a living, breathing, experiencing, desiring dynamism, as evanescent and "untranslatable" (l. 1332) as "The play of shine and shade on the trees as the supple boughs wag" (l. 27). Believing that no spoken or written sign is adequate to express the pneumatic force within, fearing that language—even poetry—may versify the self beyond recognition, Whitman ignores "Speech's" taunting sarcasms and "refuses" the reader's yearning solicitations. Not even at the end of "Song of Myself" will Whitman do anything more than encourage the reader to continue pursuing him, even though Whitman, at the same time, postpones his self-revelation: "Failing to fetch me at first keep encouraged, / Missing me one place search another, / I stop some where waiting for you" (ll. 1344–46). "Some where," but not in the poem.

That is, Whitman may be dwelling poetically somewhere in America, but not in any words. Not in Whitman's proper name, which appears only once (l. 497), and especially not in the word "I," the shifting pronoun that supposedly specifies the individual human origin of "Song of Myself" (a poem without a signature). That "I" is simply a blank identification opening the poem and automatically entangling in its pseudo-illocutionary acts another shifting pronoun, "you," which closes the poem, with no period behind it. Although the situations Whitman actually experienced, wherein an authoritative "I" (Taylor, Hicks, Alboni, and so on) entranced a rapturous "you" (always Whitman) and took place in a concrete historical context, here the I-you (Whitman-reader) situation has a divisive middle term, the written text. The text disrupts immediate involvement and abstracts the "I" and the "you" out of their particularized context. When (pro-)nominalized, the essential self, the "Me myself" celebrated by the "I" and projected toward the "you," becomes lifted out of its concrete singularity and generalized into a formal constituent of discourse.

Hence, in the words of Paul de Man, "*I* cannot say I. . . . The philosophical I is not only self-effacing, as Aristotle demanded, in the sense of being humble and inconspicuous, it is also self-effacing in the much more radical sense that the position of the I, which is the condition for thought, implies its eradication, not as in Fichte, as the symmetrical position of its negation but as the undoing, the erasure of any relationship, logical or otherwise, that could be conceived between what the I is and what it says it is."[5] The "I" is a discrete individual content, but the "I" is a universal, formal variable. To make matters worse, it is the necessary starting point in the performance of self-celebration. Furthermore, the closing ceremony rests upon the "you," the anticipated reader ideally locked in intimate communion with the "*I*." But instead of marking unique selves, the

5. Paul de Man, "Sign and Symbol in Hegel's *Aesthetics*," *Critical Inquiry*, VIII (1982), 769.

pronouns establish formal, positional functions (grammatical, not epistemological) any person may fulfill who happens to pick up *Leaves of Grass*. Just as the "I" is, in John L. Austin's speech act vocabulary, a recorded "utterance-origin," a printed grammatical subject, not the "real" Walt Whitman alive in Brooklyn in 1855, the "you" is a receiver of the utterance, the one mediately addressed who may shun the undersigned in disdain (*à la* Whittier) or subject it to an interpretation that compromises the "I's" intentions.[6] Would Whitman wish to implicate his "final merit" in this language game?

Hence Whitman maintains his recalcitrance. To submit himself, his "own physical, emotional, moral, intellectual, and aesthetic Personality" (*PW*, II, 714), to verbal signs would be to surrender himself to interpretation, to accrue unto himself more cultural clutter, to thwart the unmediated, intuitive, palpable contact he so desires. Although it previously seemed to offer Whitman a forceful oracular avenue straightway to the "Personalities" of his individual readers, language turns out to be the very impediment blocking such access.

And yet he still wants desperately to communicate. His radical critique and attempted exclusion of the linguistic middle in no way undermines his prime motivation to bond men and women in a natural communion. His desire for unity remains unaffected, as does his persistent idealization of *Leaves of Grass:* "My verse strains its very nerve to arouse, brace, dilate, excite to love & realization of health, friendship, perfection, freedom, amplitude" (*Cor*, II, 151; letter dated 1872). In order to achieve "love," what his verse must "strain" against is its verbal restraints. His words must negate themselves and become like electrical "nerves" vibrating with the touch of feeling.

This is the argument of Section 25—to develop a language, a style and a lexicon, that undermines its own linguistic properties. The poem tries to make its words point to a more natural medium than conventional talk, to compel the unavoidable verbal signs to cooperate in their own demise. That more natural medium awaiting the word's dissipation is, of course, physiognomy, the unified corporeal text Whitman opposes favorably to language: "Encompass worlds but never try to encompass me. / I crowd your noisiest talk by looking toward you" (ll. 577–78).

It may be appropriate to use speech to "encompass worlds" and "vol-

---

6. John L. Austin, *How to Do Things with Words*, ed. J. O. Urmson and Marina Sbisa (Cambridge, Mass., 1962), 60.

umes of worlds," but to use speech to realize the self only circumscribes and codifies its object. To uncover the proleptic, natural truth lurking in every soul requires a medium less opaque, conventional, and historical than language, here reduced to "noisiest talk." And so, although Whitman tells his readers that they must find themselves by themselves without his assistance, he does, nevertheless, give them negative directions, stern advice usually intended to wean them away from words and books and literary occasions. In this antidialectic, this healthy regression back to primal sympathies, the poem plays the role of a brief but indispensable starting point, a provisional meeting place that must be left behind, consigned to the shuttered library as Whitman and comrade sally off into "the open air." The actual "Writing" has little inherent worth:

> Writing and talk do not prove me,
> I carry the plenum of proof and everything else in my face,
> With the hush of my lips I confound the topmost skeptic.
>
> (ll. 579–81)

Writing is prospective; it merely points to a more natural, self-identical (non-)text, the poet's face, which silently enacts an unmediated feeling-experience in its onlookers. Notwithstanding those who decry such transports, physiognomy sits calmly secure of its mastery. A knowing "hush," what Whitman later calls "a significant look that you do not forget" ("To a Common Prostitute"), emanating from his satiate countenance discomposes the cocksure "skeptic," the wavering critical "contender" (l. 80) who scoffs at purpose and commitment and regards man's sincerest aspirations as folly.

The skeptic, a philosopher of appearance who demonstrates the untrustworthiness of the senses and advocates universal doubt or suspension of judgment concerning ontological truth, beholds, when confronted with Whitman's face, an immanent, manifest fullness, a "plenum of proof" of a different order than that achieved by discursive logic. The essence is *in* the face, there to be seen and felt, without reasoning or fact finding. As Whitman says, "The facts are useful and real....they are not my dwelling....I enter by them to an area of the dwelling" (ll. 491–92). To Emerson's skeptic, "Montaigne," who, in an effort to curb the dogmatic impulse, marks with certainty the paltry limits of human understanding, Whitman replies with a pacific, self-satisfied complacency. The poet knows that his "knowledge" exceeds those limits; indeed, that it exceeds the words he must use to express it. Writing and talk do not "prove" (read "test" or "verify") him. They merely circulate him, pass through him, and send his inscribed (and disassociated) self to others.

But physiognomy both affects others and remains connected to its origin. Although language necessitates an inadequate translation of feeling into words, physiognomy, through its natural affinity with the soul, instantaneously corresponds to feeling. And every physiognomy is unique and "personal"; it is each person's own language. Although a signifying distance may exist in the relation of feeling to face—a spatial gap between internal and external, a temporal delay between cause and effect—their topographies are congruent and the time is immeasurably quick. In adding nothing extraneous to its motivating source, in being just as individual as its origin, it never entirely forsakes its proper dwelling. Although it metamorphoses feeling into worldly forms so that it may be communicated, it does so innocently, without violating feeling's purity, without using perverse or estranging media to lure it into social discourse. The physiognomic sign is one's own, just as the feeling is one's own.

Unlike language, physiognomy incorporates many of the properties characterizing the inner life of the soul. It is natural, not fabricated; spontaneous, not calculated; unique, not reiterable. Always respecting the authority of its inception, physiognomy will not yield itself up to criticism or interpretation or any analytic practice that brings to bear upon expression an intellectual bias and arrogates to itself the determination of meaning and value. Because the organic nexus guarantees physiognomy's truth and candor, the accessory sign is dispensed with, rendered moot by the tangible facial image. The face is self-evident, therefore explanation is superfluous. Physiognomy's rightful future proves to be not another sign, but an experience that is an end in itself. With a self-present, undifferentiated, pure, and natural emotion arrived at, semiosis stops once and for all.

This concludes the poetic process. Presumably, Whitman's original inspiration has arrived at its proper destination, the reader's soul. Feeling has traversed the intermediary word with no troublesome declension. Composition and interpretation have become restricted to straightforward operations whereby signs are simply attached to and detached from emotion or from organic symbols (physiognomic sights and inarticulate sounds) contiguous with emotion. Of course, Whitman's faith in the communicative model depends upon his repression of what he already suspects about the arbitrary sign: lacking a natural determination, it may deviate from its proper course. For this reason, the productive tensions and conflicts in "Song of Myself" are due less to the very real personal problems and political ambivalences Whitman actually suffered than they are to his anxiety over words' capacity to play an innocent, momentary role in the exchange of feeling.

That anxiety manifests itself in the compromise Whitman poses here. Although his signs may not represent adequately a human essence, at least they will couple with a special category of signs marked by their organicism. Instead of delivering signs of feeling itself, he moderates his claims by wielding signs of symbols. (But what is to make the connection between sign and symbol any more certain than that between sign and feeling?)

Whitman's prevarications are contradictions, not conflicts. They do not stage a thematic opposition of ideas or beliefs. Rather, they polarize unresolvable attitudes toward the sign. That is, to Whitman, the sign is both harbinger and absentee of truth, feeling, the self. On the one hand, the poem acts as inaugurating "adhesiveness" preparing Whitman and others for a shared inspiration. On the other hand, the poem acts as a ubiquitous exterior barrier forestalling natural human interaction. To ensure the former and preclude the latter, Whitman, at the same time that he "celebrates himself," does indeed "contradict himself," speak against his vocation, underwrite and undermine his own writing. That he writes prodigiously does not contradict his attitude toward writing; for, he presumes, only through grandiloquent, effusive outbursts of poetry can the material form of verse, the extrinsic sign, be transcended. Only through a superabundance of language will the sign's disjunctive, supplementary actions become clear. Once recognized for what it is, the sign may then be disposed of.

Before and beyond this semiotic excess lies the plenary silence founding and resolving all signifying acts, the presiding but concealed identity from which words, gestures, cries, and countenances proceed and to which they properly return. As an unsignified presence calling for representation, Whitman's silent interior self is the source of all society and the measure of their truth (how accurately they satisfy their origin). Because it strays the least from its natural wellspring, physiognomy is the most proprietary and credible of signs. Though not a perfect *reflection*, it is, in Whitman's tenuous taxonomy of signs, the most minimal *deflection*. It allows Whitman, without losing himself, to recall readers to themselves. Silent and projective, physiognomy mediates faithfully between the annunciating voice and the voice that keeps silent, the words disseminated to the world and the Word resting quietly in its private domain.

These are the ideal extremes between which "Song of Myself" in theory oscillates—the unspoken, physiognomic sublime and the hyperspoken, voluminous sublime. The functioning middle realm is language, alternately the communal host binding man with nature and the institutional prison house prolonging man's seclusion. Bound by language, "Song of Myself" is both Orphic Logos and antipoem, a grand expression of the American soul and a cynical gainsaying of the expression of soul. "Song of Myself" bears in its own contradictory movements the possibilities, the triumph or pitfalls, of writing.

But what about the possibilities of reading, of its being read? What about future interpretations? What about not the written word but the registered word, the glyph passed on to generations of readers? Whether regarded as a poetry effacing its own language or as a poetry elevating language to natural purity, "Song of Myself" makes it clear that the responsibility for completing the poetic process lies with the reader rather than the creator. Faced with nothing but a "printed and bound book" (l. 1088) whose written signs only indirectly suggest a physiognomy or a voice, the reader bears the burden of transcending those technical impediments and uncovering the true poem lurking in their past (the instant of feeling and its most immediate manifestations). That past is nothing on the face of it; the past is instead the poem's future, the outcome of which decides the failure or success of Whitman's poetics. Readers must follow his signs along an undeviating pathway back to their natural beginnings. Without the reader's obedient reconstruction of the originary feeling, Whitman's poetic project remains uncompleted, and his ambition to become America's first poet, the principal guiding figure in American culture, is suspended. But, as Whitman soon realizes, in implicating "readers to come" in the workings of his poems, he subjects himself to another's will. His works become offered up to readers' intellectual or critical predispositions, not to mention their arbitrary whims and fancies, a situation he can barely tolerate. (Often when speaking to O'Connor, Traubel, and other votaries about reactions to *Leaves of Grass*, Whitman labels as "slanderer" or "enemy" anyone who takes anything less than a laudatory attitude toward his work.)

One might assume that although Whitman would object to analytical criticism, he would welcome emotional responses, even negative ones, because they spring from a natural basis and accord with the emotional freedom he advocates. But this is not the case. Although celebrating his own random moods and attitudes, Whitman fears those of others and, in fact, does all he can to guarantee that readers recuperate his original inspiration properly according to *his* ruling intentions. That is, in order to avoid becoming a victim of his own poetic-ethic, to circumscribe the critical and emotive appropriations he will allot only to himself, Whitman attempts to direct the readers' all-important interpretive backtracking into the origin of "Song of Myself." This assertion of authority, this will to control a process in which so much of himself is at stake, takes the form not only of numerous critical pieces (prefaces, essays, self-reviews, notes, and so on) with which he surrounds each edition of *Leaves of Grass*, but also, and most significantly, later poems (many from the second edition), the added contents of *Leaves of Grass*.

In the following chapters, we will see that many of the major poems appended in 1856 and 1860 function as footnotes to "Song of Myself" and ponder the future of his completed task. They ruminate upon its beginning and end, the mythical moment when Whitman first found himself using words to express feeling and the apprehensive consequences of giving those words to an audience. It is generally the poems of 1856 that underscore the latter and that we must now turn to. Those of 1860 we reserve for later, marking as they do Whitman's final withdrawal and summary undoing of what he proposes in his first and greatest poem.

3
Reading

The poem immediately following "Song of Myself" in the first edition (later called "A Song for Occupations"[1]) begins with a simple, direct entreaty:

> Come closer to me,
> Push close my lovers and take the best I possess,
> Yield closer and closer and give me the best you possess.
>
> This is unfinished business with me....how is it with you?
> I was chilled with the cold types and cylinder and wet paper between us.
>
> (ll. 1–5)

He "*was* chilled." Henceforth, we may dispose of print, paper, and other "cold" mediations and enjoy the thrilling warmth of emotive bodily contact. But even though, presumably, writing now is committed to the past—that is, to the previous poem, which has, through its self-effacing signs, carried poet and disciple beyond technique and artifice and mediation—still there remains "unfinished business." The mutual swapping of "the best," occurring only through intimate "contact of bodies and souls" (l. 6, later deleted), is still pending. Further instruction is required:

1. I quote the first version of every poem noted, but I call them by their final title.

There is something that comes home to one now and perpetually,
It is not what is printed or preached or discussed....it eludes discussion and
     print,
It is not to be put in a book....it is not in this book,
. . . .
You may read in many languages and read nothing about it;
. . . .
I do not know what it is except that it is grand, and that it is happiness,
And that the enclosing purport of us here is not a speculation, or bon-mot or
     reconnoissance,
And that it is not something which by luck may turn out well for us, and
     without luck must be a failure for us,
And not something which may yet be retracted in a certain contingency.

                                                 (ll. 44–58)

In both style and subject matter, these didactic lines parallel Section 50 of "Song of Myself," the uplifting hymnal climax wherein Whitman affirms "eternal life" and "happiness" for all "brothers and sisters." But although both passages eulogize this "perpetual" "home-like" presence in all its transcendent benevolence, what stands out in each description is its inaccessibility to language. Appearing in the first edition within a few pages of one another, both sections speak of the "grand" but unspeakable truth lying at the base of all metaphysics, deny its representation by "utterance or symbol" and "discussion and print," refer to "it" in vague, negative terms—"There is something," "I do not know what it is," "It is not"—and then give to it the frankly inadequate name "happiness" (or perhaps "happiness" is merely a signifiable concomitant of "it"). But whereas in "Song of Myself" Whitman confidently attributes "it" to himself—"There is that *in me*"—in "A Song for Occupations," he regards "happiness" objectively: "something that comes home *to one.*" Whereas the first poem emphasizes the poet's difficulty in *expressing* the "happiness" surging within him, the subsequent poem points out the impossibility of *reading* it in the word. "It is not what is printed or preached or discussed"; it is not in any language. Therefore it cannot be read or communicated in any ordinary sense of the term.

He "knows" it because it *affects* him. To Whitman, the encounter with "happiness" is a moment of nonlinguistic seizure by some organic medium of presence (call it "magnetism," "vocalism," "*live feeling*," and so on), an arresting penetration that overrides human will and permeates the soul. Conversely, reading, in his view, involves a calculated interpretation of lifeless transmissions no longer continuous with their authoritative provenance, an attempt to decipher original feelings from their exterior, errant representations. If those signs turn out to be inadequate to their source or if the reader lacks the necessary sensitivity and native breadth, reading will degenerate into critical appropriations more or less responsive to the poet's creative impulse, "leaving each reader eligible to form the resultant-poem for herself or himself" (*NUPM*, I, 335). Notwithstanding the language's magnetic attraction, its intended effect is left to the reader's arbitrary choice. In consequence, reading is indeterminate, a matter of chance, "something which by luck may turn out well for us, and without luck must be a failure for us."

Rather than letting *ananke* lapse into *tyche*, rather than offering up his inviolate, soul-inspired songs to capricious interpretations, Whitman insists that "the enclosing purport of us here is not a *speculation*, or *bon-mot* or *reconnoissance*." This italicized grouping names three types of reading that do violence to what is given, what is natural, what lives in the present. Specifically, "speculation," financially considered, is a self-serving projection into an unknown, random future, an investment of the signs of one's resources into a fluctuating, ineffable marketplace of percentages and interest rates and gains and losses, an attempt to take account of innumerable variables to add to one's store of possessions. Philosophically considered, speculation relinquishes concrete reality for the airy heights of abstraction and pursues absolute knowledge, theory, and proof, not realizing that the answer lies in the ground below: "I swear there can be no theory of any account, unless it corroborate the theory of the earth!" ("A Song of the Rolling Earth," l. 93).

A "bon-mot"—a literary parody of "the password primeval"—is the condensed result of "dandified" criticism, a witty epithet encapsulating but trivializing profound, sublime utterance (for example, Kenneth Burke calling Emerson's *Nature* a "Happiness Pill"). A "bon-mot" converts inspiration into the pithy phrase admirable more for its nifty sounds or clever ironies than for its sincere and direct meaningfulness.

And "reconnoissance"—that is, "scouting ahead," reading beyond the due confines of poem and poet—forsakes the proper locus of feeling and truth for pointless, extravagant meanderings into future representations. In other words, "*speculation*, or *bon-mot* or *reconnoissance*" needlessly supplements Whitman's language of the soul and adds to it irrespective of its organic wholeness. A proper reception of *Leaves of Grass* pays heed to "the law of [Whitman's] own poems" (*PW*, I, 210) and "tallies" faithfully their emotive permutations, lives and breathes in harmony with Whitman's "respiration and inspiration.... the beating of [his] heart" ("Song of Myself, " l. 23), and thus incorporates his "meaning" directly, without alteration or "contingency." Unlike ordinary discourse, which can be refuted by arguments, disproved by facts, or qualified by future discourse, Whitman's poetry, once circulated, cannot be modified or "retracted" by inhospitable readers. His words carry feeling vigorously and ineluctably to those whose hearts are primed for it, those who need not "read" in order to understand.

These are Whitman's ideal (non-)readers, the "yous" whom he addresses in so many of the poems following in the wake of "Song of Myself." Indeed, apart from the tiresome catalog poems commemorating democratic life in the New World, the most prevalent motif in the second and third editions is that of Whitman, with more or less trepidation, counseling readers in how to interpret his poems. As in "A Song for Occupations," he usually expresses his acute consciousness of coming interpreters, of "Whoever You Are Holding Me Now in Hand," and then advises them to turn off their analytic apparatus and free themselves for an immediate, palpable incursion of emotive magnetism. He admits, "I know very well these [poems] may have to be searched many times before they come to you and comply with you. / But what of that? Has not Nature to be searched many times?" (*NUPM*, I, 263).

This preoccupation with reading marks a considerable step beyond the major issue of "Song of Myself"—composition—although both develop out of Whitman's disquiet over the arbitrariness of the sign. Supposedly having surmounted "writerly" mediations in his preparatory epic, Whitman considers next the other side of communication—response. "Song of Myself" initiated Whitman's flight from the arbitrary sign by exploring the possibility of writing a natural language of pure sound or physiognomy; successive poems extend his "language experiment" by attempting to circumscribe not the inscription itself but its reception. Reading, not composition, becomes the central concern of Whitman's poetics, the dominant anxiety revealed by numerous explicit directives and supplications to far-off anticipated readers:

Whoever you are, now I place my hand upon you, that you be my poem,
I whisper with my lips close to your ear,
I have loved many women and men, but I love none better than you.
O I have been dilatory and dumb,
I should have made my way straight to you long ago,
I should have blabbed nothing but you, I should have chanted nothing but you.
("To You," ll. 6–11)

Let the paper remain on the desk unwritten, and the book on the shelf
unopened! ("Song of the Open Road," l. 216)

You bards of ages hence! when you refer to me, mind not so much my poems,
Nor speak of me that I prophesied of The States, and led them the way of their
glories;
But come, I will take you down underneath this impassive exterior—I will tell
you what to say of me:
Publish my name and hang up my picture as that of the tenderest lover,
The friend, the lover's portrait, of whom his friend, his lover was fondest,
Who was not proud of his songs, but of the measureless ocean of love within
him—and freely poured it forth . . . ("Recorders Ages Hence," ll. 1–5;
the second line was later deleted.)

I am a man who, sauntering along, without fully stopping, turns a casual look
upon you and then averts his face,
Leaving it to you to prove and define it,
Expecting the main things from you. ("Poets to Come," ll. 7–9)

See, projected through time,
For me, an audience interminable.
With firm and regular step they wend—they never stop,
Successions of men . . .
With faces turned sideways or backward toward me to listen,
With eyes retrospective towards me. ("Starting from Paumanok, ll. 29–36)

I myself make the only growth by which I can be appreciated,
I reject none, accept all, reproduce all in my own forms. ("By Blue Ontario's
Shore," ll. 10–11)

To this list of verse passages dealing with the prospects of reading, one
could add dozens of quotations from Whitman's various prose writings.
For example, he writes, "I suppose it is hardly necessary to tell you that I
have *pitched* and *keyed* my pieces more with reference to fifty years

hence, & how they will stand mellowed and toned *then*—than to pleasing & tickling the immediate impressions of the present hour" (*Cor*, II, 310). This rejection of "immediate impressions" and admission of rhetorical calculation, written in 1874, shows the extent to which Whitman has modified his poetics.

One recognizes in the lines above several Whitmanian strategies abounding in the 1856 and 1860 editions. In the first quotation, Whitman, on the one hand, desires to inseminate readers with his seductive "lispings," to make them one with his poems, and, on the other hand, he fears that his "chant," too self-centered and peculiar, falls on benumbed ears. In the second, he tells readers to cast away their books and pens and join the bard on the open road (theoretically, the last thing Whitman wants readers to do is produce more writing) and apprehend with him "something better than any and all books, and that is the real stuff whereof they are the artificial transcript and portraiture" (*NUPM*, I, 188). In the third, he sets clear-cut prescriptions for future poets and critics to consult when memorializing him and his poems. In the fourth, he places responsibility on readers to complete his poems, "to prove and define" the inarticulate feelings he has rendered to them, although he will, in fact, denounce their results, a reaction not merely whimsical and personal but entirely consistent with his anticritical poetics. In the fifth, he positions himself at the head of a genealogy of "men-poets" who maintain a venerating attitude toward their patriarchal origin. And finally, he casts himself as "the only growth," the only aesthetic guideline or evaluative criterion, by which his poems are to be judged.

The various references or intentions here all share a common provocation—the anxiety of misreading. Because every expression is complete only after it has made its intended *impression*, Whitman's ideal poetic communication of soul and feeling rests on proper reading just as much as it does on proper composing. His poetics compasses two sites: the poet "auto-graphing" the blank paper, inscribing feeling into notation; and the reader de-inscribing the printed page, lifting the embedded content up into its ideal emotive sphere. The first scene the poet can moderately control; the second he cannot. This is especially distressing to Whitman; for, having burdened the sign with so much "meaning," having charged his words not merely with representing other words but with administering the impenetrable depths of his soul, he thereby implicates not only his poems but also himself personally in every act of reading. What if his language has too little poetic-emotive power to override readers' critical biases and probe their enclothed souls? What if nineteenth-century American literary culture proves too canonical and exclusive to tolerate any radical departures from its stylistic and material norms? What if the sign is such only according to its interpretation, not its intention?

First, one might ask why reading comes to assume so prominent a place among Whitman's concerns, and why writing, which was predominate in "Song of Myself," seems to become a secondary issue? Early in 1856, with his first effort having been printed and distributed and reviewed (with wildly mixed results), Whitman suddenly finds himself entangled in the vagaries of reader responses, baffled and dismayed and angered by imputations of licentiousness, stupidity, and impiety (notwithstanding his liberalism, Whitman maintained a deep puritanical conviction regarding many moral and religious questions), and immensely elated by expressions of favor and thanks (by Emerson, Charles Eliot Norton, Moncure Conway, Fanny Fern, and others). Relishing any praise he received (he carried Emerson's letter in his pocket for months), he felt emboldened to even more power over his audience. In one sense, the huge satisfaction Whitman got from positive notices made him realize just how important reception was to him. They caused him almost as much anxiety as the negative responses.

As to the "insults," Whitman was somewhat at a loss to explain how a volume overflowing with "happiness" and "love" could evoke abuse. What knowledge or custom or faculty stood in the way of mutual enjoyment? Why did readers adopt such fruitless skeptical habits? Where did they learn to interpret altruism as narcissism, joy as hedonism, and sentiment as sentimentality? Something unaccountable (and unnatural) must be at work in certain interpretations—something, he thought, that sympathy and compassion could not contend with. If so, then more passion poetry, more democratic celebrations, would only excite more vilification. Hence he initiates his notorious self-promotions and partisan criticisms, polemical gestures that engage hostile criticism on its own malevolent terms.

Seeing Whitman placed firmly in the canon, modern scholars regard his attacks and defenses and inverted plagiarisms (that is, passing his own evaluative statements off as someone else's) as an embarrassing and pathetic spectacle. But to the poet in 1856, ambitious for fame, presuming to be the voice of America, and obsessed with his reputation, the thought of misconstruction, of biased judgments of his private merits and unfair characterizations of his poems, fills him with despair and drives him into these literary hoaxes.

It is true that, as many point out, praise from Emerson, Alcott, Thoreau, and others marked a high moment in Whitman's life and probably encouraged him to try to master his readers. But still, their responses fell short of the universal welcome he envisioned. They convinced him he was "right" and hostile critics were "wrong," but that only indicated further cultural division, the very antagonism Whitman wished to end.

For him, then, the question is not one of ethics, but one of rhetoric: Will his criticism influence his reception any better than his poetry? Will criticism make future interpretations any more congenial than present ones? Based upon his first experience of critical reviews, the outlook is uncertain; for, having endured the fickle assessments of public scrutiny, Whitman can easily project himself into a distant future in which *Leaves of Grass* is merely a pawn in a conflict of interpretations past and present. Then, there will not even be an author to authorize revision and counterattack and ghostwriting, no living origin to guarantee the right response to his work. His self-criticism will stand merely as one interpretation among many others (was there ever a time when it did not?).

At that point, only his poems will speak for him. To do so effectively, they must manifest his presence palpably and reliably, magnetically enough to preclude analysis and silence criticism, vigorously enough to substantiate Whitman's claim that "this is no book—but I myself, in loving flesh and blood" (*NUPM*, IV, 1465). But, as Whitman realizes in 1856, poetry is not enough; ultimately, it is the reader who vindicates the poet. No matter how much his language succeeds in transmigrating his living soul across "vast trackless spaces . . . projected through time" ("Starting from Paumanok," ll. 25 and 29), if it does not evoke a corresponding feeling or experience in the reader's soul, if it is unable to exact an immediate intuitive affirmation of truth and empathy, the poem has failed.

Although Whitman's songs come from the heart, readers still may condemn them as the formless sentiments of an unskilled hack, the bestial bellowings of an uncultured brute, and banish them from literary discourse. In other words, culling an array of natural, transparent signs from the rampant dross of conventional literary language in order to found a natural poetic language appropriate to the human soul only raises another problem, one less governable than that of the poet's choice of words—the possibility of *natural reading*. That question forces itself upon Whitman when he turns his attention to posterity, when he realizes that the future of *Leaves of Grass* depends not upon particular truths being discovered and memorialized (who Walt Whitman was, what was happening in Brooklyn in the 1850s, what experiences or beliefs motivated this or that poem, and so on), but instead upon the vicissitudes of interpretation, upon the inconstant and uncontrollable reception of the sign, upon reading correctly or incorrectly the scattered traces of Whitman's being.

A correct reading would, of course, follow the natural guidelines (yet another oxymoron) Whitman sketches variously in his poetry and prose. He assumes that "his contempt for the 'poets' and 'poetry' of the day, his presentation of thoughts and things at first hand, instead of second or third hand, his sturdy and old-fashioned earnestness, and his unprecedented novelty, make him a capitol target for the smart writers and verbal fops engaged in manufacturing items and 'criticism'." So, "like all revolutionists and founders, he himself will have to create the growth by which he is to be fully understood and accepted" (*NUPM*, II, 898–99[2]). Because Whitman presents "thoughts and things at first hand," without stock ornamentation, the "smart writers and verbal fops" who dominate the literary milieu and believe such adornments to be the essence of poetry can only ridicule him with "slur, burlesque, and sometimes spiteful innuendo." Or they "emasculate" Whitman by turning *Leaves of Grass* into a mere topic of polite conversation, a poetic subject to be bandied about: "A talent for conversation—Have you it? If you have, you have a facile and dangerous tenant in your soul's palace" (*NUPM*, I, 295).

In either case, these glib reviewers degrade inspired poetry, dismissing it because inspiration is un- or pre-aesthetic. It is up to Whitman to vanquish readers who praise or blame according to a poet's skill in handling literary conventions and who rest content in limiting their analyses to the level of decorum instead of delving into the underlying feeling. He himself must bear the responsibility of fostering the "growth" of natural reading and carving out his own fit audience (although, in the same para-

2. Whitman assumes the third person here, even though he is writing about himself, because these phrases come from notes for one of his anonymous self-promotions. This particular scrap dates from late 1871 and is intended as a defense of his public reading of "As a Strong Bird on Pinions Free."

graph, Whitman notes his own "scornful silence, never explaining any-thing, nor answering any attack," a strategy he scarcely adhered to from 1855 onward).

To promote natural reading, Whitman first must break readers of their conventional "Book-learning" habits of inquiry and reorient them to the proper way of reading and experiencing nature. Put simply, a natural reading of Whitman's poetry would repeat, on the reader's part, the same experience Whitman has when he interacts with nature. His "poems . . . [are] to be perceived with the same perception that enjoys music, flowers, and the beauty of men and women" (*NUPM*, IV, 1443). The physical exhilaration he felt when listening to Alboni sing Verdi (see *PW*, II, 694), the desire to coalesce with eternity that draws him to the sea, where, he says, "I wended the shores I know, / As I walked with that eternal self of me, seeking types" ("As I Ebb'd with the Ocean of Life," ll. 16–17), the passive inquisitiveness leading him to bend "with open eyes over the shut eyes of sleepers" ("The Sleepers," l. 3) and enter into their dreams and nightmares—all such natural impulses and responses should moti-vate and delimit a proper reading of *Leaves of Grass*.

Readers should approach Whitman's poetic language as they do the sensuous living language of leaves and rivers and sunshine, of human countenances and slang speech, real-life signs that are reacted to with all one's being. The true language of life can be touched, tasted, and smelled, as well as heard and seen:

Earth round, rolling, compact—suns, moons, animals—all these are words,
Watery, vegetable, sauroid advances—beings, premonitions, lispings of the
    future—these are vast words.
Were you thinking that those were the words—those upright lines? Those
    curves, angles, dots?
No, those are not the words—the substantial words are in the ground and sea,
They are in the air—they are in you.
                            ("A Song of the Rolling Earth," ll. 2–4;
                            the first two lines were deleted after 1871.)

A reading focused upon "curves, angles, dots," upon print's uniform black and white, confines itself to a textual configuration and checks the kind of feeling interaction Whitman faithfully proposes between author and reader. Instead of attending to human origins, reading lapses into mere decoding, into translating prosaically these imageless stick figures back into their perceptible references and then evaluating the poet's "invention," *his* poetic translation of certain ideas or truths into verse. Scholarly or dilettante readers approach poetry by studying linguistic embellishments of the things themselves and classifying a work, usually from the perspective of a restrictive literary history, according to its superficialities (its decorum, poetic diction, obedience to "unities," and so on). Instead of incorporating "beings" and "premonitions," they merely annotate a text and leave those "substantial words," the realities, untouched. Whitman would often righteously point out to his adoring votaries how far their idle criticism deviates from an honest human apprehension of nature's wonders!

He also suggests that these pale men of letters read and write in such an abstract, irrelevent manner not only because of local socio-historical factors but because of linguistic conditions as well. Instead of blaming perverse reading practices simply on arid scholarly influences and the imaginative defects of routine readers, Whitman also censures the representational distance between percept and sound and sound and script. He condemns any sign that makes possible interpretive errancy, which cushions the immediate sensible impact of natural phenomena and screens individuals from a direct intuition of feeling. The tenuous progress from perception to print, from image to sound to letter, is, of course, prone to the mischievous effects of translation, not only to the translator's interestedness and ideological slant but to translation itself, the leap from one sign system to another, which necessarily works transformative operations upon its "content." In simple terms, with every translation, that content is adapted to a new grammar—that is, a new temporality, spatiality, history, and so on—undergoing resignification that amounts more to a mutation than an adaptation.

Only a privileged few have the natural genius and selflessness either to withstand the seductions that this dangerous substitution offers or at least to render it innocuous and read the sign aright. They form with Whitman an inner circle of interpreters, "a conference amid Nature, and in the spirit of nature's genesis, and primal sanity. A conference of [their] two Souls exclusively, as if the rest of the world, with its mocking misconceptions were for a while left and escaped from" (*NUPM*, IV, 1452). The stinging prevalence of "criticism" and "mocking misconceptions" in his social and literary worlds causes Whitman to demand that readers school themselves in the language of nature, the "vast . . . substantial words" comprising the universal poem. Though textual—the "Earth," "suns, moons, animals," "ground and sea," "air," and "you" *are* "words"—their meaning is unique and immanent, unequivocally there for our physical and emotional pleasure, not for our intellectual wit and discernment. "Words" of/in nature are not traces; they are unified entities.

Composition reorders and resignifies those self-evident materializations of truth or spirit, imposing a secondary, man-made textual machination upon nature's sensuous presentations. It thus impoverishes the colorful display of beauty and warmth by submitting it to a skeletal notation. Too often, instead of rescuing nature and all its sublime manifestations from composition's excesses, reading only produces more outward signs, more camouflaging layers of artifice. Conventional reading proliferates verbiage and thus fosters the linguistic departure from nature. Natural reading, however, produces (or, rather, reproduces) nothing more than what is there. Much like his own restless attempt to translate the "meanings" of nature (albeit an effort he often regards as faulty) and opposed to his critics' arrogant, treacherous attempt to translate the "meanings" of his poems, natural reading retains an innocent, subdued receptivity to the pure thing before it. It halts any modifying tendencies. It constitutes both the poetic language and its interpretive (non-)methods as transparent—the former a vehicle of feeling, the latter a passive admittance of feeling. As a result, the poem remains intact, free to work its emotive power on and in its own terms without being mutated into an alien language.

This is, for Whitman, the preferred reading situation, the natural context wherein readers commune with writers and accommodate themselves to writers' passionate turns and innovations. The book functions as a provisional gathering place or scene of reading that suspends interpretation. Ideally, readers perceive without analyzing, apprehend without judging, repeat without annotating, experience texts viscerally, and leave interpretation to critics caught up in the trivial game of classification and exegesis. As the poet would have it, by its distorting and generally self-serving actions, interpretation undermines a healthy, rightful appreciation of life, of the "miracles" of "Seeing hearing and feeling" ("Song of Myself," l. 523) and the bare "things" in which "All truths wait" (l. 648). When Whitman stands and faces the sublime limitlessness of earth and sky or the "democratic average" of American society, the sea off the shores of Paumanok or Broadway at noon, he simply allows their sights and sounds to pour into his exposed senses. When recording his impressions, he assumes the voice of nature and America and merely echoes ingenuously the tangible "words" they spoke to him before. When readers come upon that voice, they are to respond in the same noninterpretive, spongelike way that Whitman did when he sauntered along the beach or down the avenue, except that instead of becoming another voice of nature, readers are to become the voice of *Leaves of Grass* (Whitman would say they are one and the same), sounding in a unitary paean the natural truths therein.

Presiding over a sensuous, uninterpreted world and an undomesticated society, addressing a familiar gathering of sympathetic confreres, the poet serves as "the answerer," the irrefutable "sayer" who bears the Logos. He is the purveyor of truth—"He puts things in their attitudes" ("Song of the Answerer," l. 18)—and the arbiter of conflict—"Him all wait for....him all yield up to....his word is decisive and final" (l. 8). He gains access to private passion—"He has the passkey of hearts" (l. 28)—and he levels social rank—"The gentleman of perfect blood acknowledges his perfect blood, / The insulter, the prostitute, the angry person, the beggar, see themselves in the ways of him....he strangely transmutes them" (ll. 50–51). The "answerer" legislates and inspires, mirrors and "transmutes," in each case serving to naturalize relations, to bring the deviant back to purity. His power to compel an audience to "yield" or "acknowledge" and his capacity to "settle justice, reality, immortality" (l. 58) lie mainly in his ability to propagate faithfully and adequately the language of nature:

Every existence has its idiom....every thing has an idiom and tongue;
He resolves all tongues into his own and bestows it upon men..and·any man
    translates..and any man translates himself also:
One part does not counteract another part....He is the joiner....he sees how
    they join.

                                                 (ll. 31–33)

The poet-answerer "resolves" particularized local idioms into the universal voice of being and "bestows it upon men" who "translate" it back into a personal, idiosyncratic language. This Babel-like fragmentation, however, does not dissever the communal bond, for the poet (as "joiner") holds individuals together, reminds them of their common cause, and keeps them unified and compassionate by wielding a vernacular glue. He has "all lives, all effects, all hidden invisibly in [him]self" (*NUPM*, I, 239). "Behind [his] talk stands the real life of all who hear [him] now" (*NUPM*, IV, 2047), and so he remains the oracle to whom those who seek truth and comfort appeal. The mediator and focal point of man and man, and man and nature, he gives vent to what all feel and touch and see and love, and makes interpretation and conventional reading an encumbrance.

But what presuppositions does this scheme of pure reading rest upon? The first presuppositions is that objects or "real life," whether natural or invented, can be perceived as extralinguistic givens immediately present to the senses or as discrete identities manifesting themselves apart from any system of reference. Second, there is the assumption that voice works no instrumental changes upon what it describes, and that it represents adequately and transparently the nonlinguistic reality inspiring it. The third presupposition is that translation either from sensation to language or from one language to another occurs without deforming the original referent, that the substitution of one sign for another may be smooth and innocent. And fourth, it is assumed that readers will be willing to adopt this reading attitude against interpretation and welcome *Leaves of Grass* as they would experience ordinary natural phenomena. "Song of Myself," being Whitman's struggle to preserve natural expression during the composition process, investigates the first three issues, resolving them through a metaphysics of perception and expression. Many later poems, involving his struggle to ensure a natural perception during the reading process, also ponder the first three, but from the explicit, anxiety-ridden perspective of the fourth issue, treating it as a problem of ideology (though this in no way excludes metaphysics).

Given Whitman's desire to found a natural language of feeling and his acute understanding of the dangers of reading, his anxiety makes perfect sense. It also makes more poems. Never one to flee from his distresses without first writing about them (directly or indirectly), Whitman converts his anxiety into more poetic material, more ideas and feelings to express, deny, analyze, metamorphose, subdue, and appease. One could, as some have, group together Whitman's polemical utterances against interpretation and perform a thematic reading of them, paraphrasing his statements in a critical vocabulary and extrapolating their general content, even though many of them are already so categorically critical that they baffle any translation from their putatively creative mode.

But whereas a thematic analysis, be it psychological, political, or philosophical, might furnish students of *Leaves of Grass* with certain interests and ideas preoccupying Whitman during his lifetime, it would not reveal the textual transfigurations those "real" concerns undergo both during composition, when they leave the cloudy, ephemeral space of Whitman's mind and assume definite shape in the book, and during reading, when the reverse process takes place. "Song of Myself" probes the former, later poems the latter, but not only in a thematizing manner. Instead of simply allegorizing, in the conventional sense, a preexistent content in a narrative or image, instead of simply constructing a poetic equivalent of truth, "Song of Myself" and succeeding poems dramatize that construction, recounting the poet's search for and readers' acceptance of natural signs. That is, Whitman gives his language a performative as well as a cognitive dimension, staging repeatedly scenes of writing and reading, and these scenes question the very nature of translation. They pose in a much more forceful and interesting way than do the abstract statements against active interpretation (which themselves must be subject to interpretation) the fate of reading, its inevitable *clinamen* from authorial intention.

In examining Whitman's canon, it is easy to find dozens of reading situations, moments where the poet scans a landscape or physiognomy for its "meaning," but such scenes are difficult to analyze because they so often appear in conjunction with explicit renunciations of reading. In "Song of the Open Road," for example, Whitman declares, "You road I travel and look around! I believe you are not all that is here! / I believe that something unseen is also here" (ll. 16–17). He goes on to ponder the "objects that call from diffusion [his] meanings and give them shape!" (l. 26) and to realize that they "express [him] better than [he] can express [him]self" (l. 47). That is to say, the "open road" is a numinous text made up of seen and "unseen," material sign and spiritual "meaning," the human truth Whitman treasures but which, though it dwells in his own soul, he can apprehend only by reading it through the object. Initiating the coalescence of a subject with an object and, ultimately, with itself, reading, then, is a fortuitous moment in an emotive dialectic, a natural step on the "open road" to contentment and "Happiness."

In these phrases, there seems to be no worry over any possible missteps reading might lead one into. And yet, a few lines earlier, Whitman writes, he is "Done with indoor complaints, libraries, querulous criticisms" (l. 6). But how else to characterize his approach to nature and its latent "meanings" than as "querulous" inquisitiveness, his attacks upon "philosophies and religions" (l. 83) and "the preacher preach[ing] in his pulpit! . . . the lawyer plead[ing] in the court, and the judge expound-[ing] the law" (l. 219) as defensive, contemptuous "criticism"? To save the poet from contradiction (on this issue Whitman wishes to be decidedly consistent), we must accept Whitman's differentiation between the kind of reading that is carried out in "libraries" from that which he performs in nature. As we have seen, it would appear that the reading of books, of verbal signs arranged horizontally on pallid leaves of paper, is to be qualitatively distinguished from the reading of natural objects, of tangible things that invite participation in their actions.

To understand why Whitman considers such a distinction necessary, we turn to "Crossing Brooklyn Ferry" (originally entitled "Sun-Down Poem"), not only the most profound and sustained lyric of the 1856 poems (the one Thoreau singled out, along with "Song of Myself," as Whitman at his best) but also the poem most clearly about reading.[3] With its Heraclitean waters and Wordsworthian sunsets, its poignant apostrophes to "you who peruse me" (l. 112) a hundred years hence, and its lament for the "bitter hug of mortality" ("Song of Myself," l. 1288)— "myself disintegrated, every one disintegrated" ("Crossing," l. 7)—the poem overtly addresses the temporal human predicament and its tragic effects: aging, loss, death, oblivion.

Yet, what stands out in "Crossing Brooklyn Ferry" are not Whitman's ethical or philosophical conclusions regarding the human condition, but rather his articulation of the question of reading and what role it plays in

3. For critical readings of "Crossing Brooklyn Ferry," see Miller, *Walt Whitman's Poetry*, 199–208; Quentin Anderson, *The Imperial Self: An Essay in American Literary and Cultural History* (New York, 1971), 119–65; Black, *Whitman's Journeys into Chaos*, 157–66; Thomas, *The Lunar Light of Whitman's Poetry*, 92–116; Hollis, *Language and Style in "Leaves of Grass,"* 100–106; Joseph G. Kronick, *American Poetics of History: From Emerson to the Moderns* (Baton Rouge, 1984), 106–17; and Larson, *Whitman's Drama of Consensus*, 8–13.

an individual's development and in human history. Specifically, in the hope that it will assuage the dread of annihilation (as well as the threat of misinterpretation, which is annihilation for a poet), the poem tries to establish a comforting, stable identification between the way future generations, "you that shall cross from shore to shore years hence" (l. 5), perceive the scene and the way Whitman does in the poem:

> It avails not, neither time nor place—distance avails not,
> I am with you, you men and women of a generation, or ever so many
>   generations hence,
> I project myself, also I return—I am with you, and know how it is.
> Just as you feel when you look on the river and sky, so I felt,
> Just as any of you is one of a living crowd, I was one of a crowd,
> Just as you are refreshed by the gladness of the river, and the bright flow, I
>   was refreshed,
> Just as you stand and lean on the rail, yet hurry with the swift current, I
>   stood, yet was hurried,
> Just as you look on the numberless masts of ships, and the thick-stemmed
>   pipes of steamboats, I looked.
>   (ll. 20–26; the third line was later deleted.)

Through this imaginative amalgam of souls all correspondingly taking in the landscape, Whitman's sensations, already fading into memories that must be recorded in order to endure, are rescued from mutability and obliteration. If their reading of Brooklyn at twilight, of the river, the boats and passengers, parallels his own (and if the poem about his reading is kept in mind), then the poet escapes misinterpretation. His experiences will become their experiences. The thoughts and feelings he suffers at the transitory crossing moment from the "tall masts of Mannahatta!" to "the beautiful hills of Brooklyn!" (l. 105), from day to night, from "The similitudes of the past [to] those of the future" (l. 8), from life to death, readers also will suffer. They, too, will see their reflection flicker, "Diverge," and be left behind in the "fine spokes of light . . . in the sunlit water" (l. 116).

As others behold the fluctuating landscape while crossing on the ferry (or reading the poem) and relive sympathetically the poet's moving recognition of eternal becoming, a precious continuity of human experience will be established—what Whitman believes to be the true American history, he being one of its founding fathers. What sustains this continuity, as the poem makes clear, is this genealogical interpretive community's adherence to natural reading, an implicit agreement among readers to confine interpretation to the salutary limits set forth in the archetypal reading experience—Whitman on the ferry.

Whitman solidifies this orthodox chain of interpretation later in the poem, clarifying in his own mystifying terms how his reading is to be passed on to his descendants:

> Now I am curious what sight can ever be more stately and admirable to me
>   than my mast-hemm'd Manhatta, my river and sun-set, and my scallop-
>   edged waves of flood-tide, the sea-gulls oscillating their bodies, the hay-
>   boat in the twilight, and the belated lighter,
> Curious what gods can exceed these that clasp me by the hand, and with voices
>   I love call me promptly and loudly by my nighest name as I approach,
> Curious what is more subtle than this which ties me to the woman or man
>   that looks in my face,
> Which fuses me into you now, and pours my meaning into you.
> We understand, then, do we not?
> What I promised without mentioning it, have you not accepted?
> What the study could not teach—what the preaching could not accomplish is
>   accomplished, is it not?
> What the push of reading could not start is started by me personally, is it not?
>   (ll. 92–100; the last line was deleted after 1871 and
>   the preceding lines were extensively rearranged.)

These lines turn upon two traditional philosophical oppositions crucial to Whitman's metaphysical outlook: the sensible versus the intelligible (in the first stanza) and what can be intuited versus what can be spoken (in the second stanza). First, Whitman favorably opposes the vast panorama of "Manhatta," the friendly handclasps of comrades, the "vocalization" of his "nighest name," and the captivating physiognomic "look" of "the woman or man," to whatever transcendent realities may lie beyond his sight, touch, or hearing.

He wonders contentedly, What need has one of anything more than what is perceived? Why let a perverse curiosity about the ineffable spoil delight in the tangible and visible? Although the immediately present assuredly fills his entire being with warmth and comfort and security, the unperceivable can only appeal to abstract faith or pure reason, contemplative faculties assumed to provide wisdom and restrain the senses in their desire for excitement. But Whitman finds sensation true and sufficient unto itself; only the pointless supposition of a supersensible reality characterizes sensation as phenomenal delusion. In fact, he implies, it is conceptualization that deludes, that uselessly depletes the display of life and robs it of its energetic particularity in a restless pursuit of abstract, universal knowledge.

In the following stanza, Whitman favorably opposes the unutterable "meaning" that is "understood" or "accepted" (in other words, assimilated extralinguistically) to what is "mentioned," "studied," "taught," or "preached"—all of which necessitate indoctrination. Although the former achieves in fantasy a semantic copulation as the poet "pours [his] meaning into you," the latter amounts to a distanced interaction by means of the factitious intermediary, an event susceptible to all the deviations and misappropriations arising from the absence of a naturally grounded medium. By adhering to the natural conditions required for an ideal communion of souls instead of resorting to conventional social or intellectual discourses, and by infusing listeners with his unmediated vision instead of invoking its arbitrary substitute, Whitman preserves his authority and avoids becoming merely another one of the scribes. Also, what he feels and what he makes readers feel need not and cannot be uttered, for any detour of feeling through the sign inevitably fractures that feeling, de-notes its song, and no dialectical recuperation or circuitous return can restore it to purity.

Feeling cannot be communicated. Like the "Wisdom" that "cannot be passed from one having it, to another not having it" ("Song of the Open Road," l. 78), feeling can neither be articulated nor read nor interpreted. Properly secluded in the soul and remaining in its inviolate self-presence beyond representation, feeling can only be acknowledged and felt by those who already possess it, who already intuit it and need merely the promptings of mesmerizing bards to reexperience it. The sign by itself has no power to awaken feeling in others.

The sign succeeds not simply by its being fortuitously chosen by the poet and accurately interpreted by the reader, but of more importance, by its functioning as a familiar token of something mutually recognized by and already present in both participants. Reading is narcissism, the emancipating apprehension of one's own innate but culturally suppressed truth and pleasure. What saves reading from selfishness and anarchy is the fact that though each man and woman counts as "a simple, separate person" ("One's-Self I Sing," l. 1), there is a subjective Logos, a "word Democratic, the word En-Masse" (l. 2), enunciated by Whitman that taps the natural roots common to all men and women and ensures a constant reception of his poetry. Reading is corrupted not by readers giving free reign to their emotions but by their restricting emotion and allowing learned habits of interpretation to guide their responses.

Herein lies an opposition more relevant to "Crossing Brooklyn Ferry" and to Whitman's poetics than the metaphysical oppositions noted above —reading as a sympathetic fusion of souls versus reading as an active interpretation of texts. The former signifies an unmediated, living empathy of "persons," the latter a detached examination of signs. Whereas criticism expends itself in detailing the extraneous ornaments of feeling and then adding further supplementary languages to it, empathy (or "adhesiveness," "comraderie," "rapport," and so on), though it must also negotiate signs, reads them for their proper reference and returns them to their original emotive content, which lies within themselves as well as in the poet. When readers assume the correct empathic and auto-pathic posture of being openly receptive to the poet's heartfelt tones, semiosis, here a lineal descent of "meaning," remains within the purview of its creator. Representation and interpretation coincide perfectly; and the first signification, which, in Whitman's interpretive model, equals inspiration, survives through successive generations of interpreters (an ideal process that, of course, contradicts infinite semiosis and pinpoints the behaviorist problematics inhabiting Whitman's scene of reading).

But criticism honors no such ancestral regulation. Under criticism's arrogant scrutinizing, "adhesiveness" dissolves and, instead of meeting anticipated reader-disciples, the far-off but beguiled initiates he expects to "complete" the poem, the poet finds himself pitted against interrogating judges weighing his thoughts and words against their own capricious beliefs.

Faced with a philistine literary establishment, Whitman is obliged to reply to with conscientious disdain or to accept with smothered resentment other people's interpretations, their manipulation of his works to suit their convenience. Whitman's lies and schemes, the arrant manner in which he anonymously defends himself or uses his disciples to lead the fight against his "enemies," are sometimes despicable, sometimes pitiful. But they also indicate Whitman's sense of just how much is at stake in the way his poems are read. Irony would perhaps be a more effective means of coping with his disfiguration at the hands of shallow, unfeeling critics; but irony would force Whitman to disjoin himself from what he speaks, to exploit the incongruity between the language of the heart and the language of society, the very discrepancy between feeling and sign that set the poet up for misinterpretation in the first place.

For Whitman to employ the sign fraudulently and break the organic contiguity of soul and sound would be, of course, to violate his first commandment—to speak forthrightly, without calculation or imitation. As he says, "All poems, or any other expressions of literature, that do not tally with their writers actual life and knowledge, are lies" (NUPM, I, 265; "tally" here signifies a direct, isomorphic transition from feeling to sign). He prefers to keep his signs "personal" (although to claim to do so, he must overlook the fact that many of his writings appear beneath the disguise of another's signature), to express himself in a language subjectively especial enough to retain its unique human origin. If Whitman can adapt a social, democratic medium of communication to his idiosyncratic feelings, and prevent the reverse from happening, then reading will be not a disinterested interpretation situating the text within the main currents of contemporary literary discourse, but rather a compassionate understanding between inspired souls, an encounter that secures the unbroken pedigree of "divine literati" in the American grain.

This raises for Whitman (and for de Tocqueville) the fundamental dilemma facing the American poet: How can a unique subjective language, a language with its own personal grammar and history, be a medium of communication readily understood by others? Only when the "other" is identical to the poet will such a language have its proper effect; but if this is the case, then the poet is not a unique individual but rather an anonymous constituent of the "en masse." Consequently, the attempt to be a poet and the raw materials of poetry threaten the very singularity of selfhood that leads one to be a poet in the first place. When in practice, when trying to share his experiences and opinions with others, the poet in America always finds himself seduced into conformity, accommodating his identity to the least common denominator of democratic intersubjectivity—ordinary language.

What elevates that line of descent above compromise is the enduring presence of Whitman himself: "I and mine do not convince by arguments, similes, rhymes / We convince by our presence" ("Song of the Open Road," ll. 138–39). His constant nearness, not merely his printed words, keeps American history universal and uncommon: "What the push of reading could not start is started by me personally, is it not?" Reading must be grounded in his "person," in his soul and voice and flesh, not in the borrowed language that renders his "person" to absent readers. As Whitman says midway in *Democratic Vistas,* "If we think of it, what does civilization itself rest upon—and what object has it, with its religions, arts, school, &c., but rich, luxuriant, varied Personalism?" (*PW,* II, 392). A paragraph earlier, he writes, "[Personalism] is individuality, the pride and centripetal isolation of a human being in himself—," a "second principle" complementing "democracy, the leveler, the unyielding principle of the average."

"Personalism" respects the value and integrity of the individual soul and, although promoting community, protects the soul from a stifling submergence in the homogenous mass of democratic society. Under the humane guidelines of "personalism," reading regards the book as merely a preliminary entryway opening into an easeful inner sanctum where more intimate recognition takes place. It makes a comforting harbor of passion and truth where "the meal [is] pleasantly set" and the poet "tell[s] things in confidence" ("Song of Myself," ll. 372 and 387). This is the rightful setting of interpretation. Presided over by Whitman's "person," his "life's hot pulsing blood, / The personal urge and form for [him]—not merely paper, automatic type and ink . . ." ("Now Precedent Songs, Farewell," ll. 9–10), reading inalterably fixes upon its true subject, the heart and soul, where falsification and misinterpretation are impossible.

But what if the "Personalism" Whitman extols as the guarantor of individualism in mass society degenerates into self-absorption and disregard for the natural covenant of mankind? What if the signs available to statesmen and orators and poets, those who supply the cohesive validating myths to the community, prove to have a divisive rather than a unifying effect, leaving individuals introspective and frustrated, helplessly intent upon their souls' unrealized evolution? What if the only alternative to interpretation is noncommunication? Without a natural language, at once both universal and personal, to sustain a fluid transition from private desire to public good and to ground individual identity in a collective identity, "Personalism" collapses into solipsism. Signs and feelings are not exchanged; instead, they are reflected back to their source. The "Personal" soul, elsewhere a sensitive interpersonal constancy but here an ego engrossed in its own feelings, threatens to reduce the democratic community to Narcissus' clear pool in which each person makes love to his or her own self-projection.

Showing more critical awareness than many of his early critics, Whitman blankly confronts this possibility in "A Song of the Rolling Earth":

Each man to himself, and each woman to herself, is the word of the past and
   present, and the true word of immortality,
Not one can acquire it for another—not one!
Not one can grow for another—not one!

The song is to the singer, and comes back most to him,
The teaching is to the teacher, and comes back most to him,
The murder is to the murderer, and comes back most to him,
The theft is to the thief, and comes back most to him,
The love is to the lover, and comes back most to him,
The gift is to the giver, and comes back most to him—it cannot fail,
The oration is to the orator, and the acting is to the actor and actress, not to
   the audience,
And no man understands any greatness or goodness but his own, or the
   indication of his own.

(ll. 78–89)

The lines leading up to this passage—"The divine ship sails the divine sea for you" (l. 74); "For none more than you is immortality" (l. 78)—suggest that Whitman is here celebrating in others the same narcissistic exuberance that led him earlier to celebrate himself. But whereas in "Song of Myself" Whitman's regressive excursions into self-centeredness are generally preceded or followed by unreserved outbreaks of gregariousness, in these lines from the next to last poem in the 1856 edition, self-centeredness continues unabated. Formerly, Whitman's seclusion was accentuated by a profound silence that seemed tantalizingly to withhold the truth, but here it is the attempt to break that silence, to "teach" or "give," that creates his seclusion. Even singing and oratory, two of Whitman's preferred forms of discourse, only confirm man's entrapment within either a subjective nutshell or a prison house of language: "no man understands any greatness or goodness but his own, or the indication of his own." The speech or behavior intended to silence debate, appease dissension, and harmonize opposing parties into a community of visionaries unconsciously acknowledging the natural foundations of democratic fellowship no longer has the power to do so. Indeed, action has fallen into crime—murder, rioting, slavery, expansionism—and language has only aggravated dispute and made government a matter of compromise. Because every utterance and every action returns to its origin without having truly engaged the souls of its "audience," communication (in Whitman's ideal sense) can never take place. And because the democratic community rests upon a self-projected communication, the self-interest resulting from this monologic practice undermines any firm beliefs in American ideals and corrupts American society.

To appreciate the extent and gravity of this conclusion, we must remember that it had been Whitman's proclaimed cardinal purpose to arrest this decline and reinstitute those natural truths and rights that the New World experiment properly rested upon. But to rejuvenate the primitive brotherhood of man required, in Whitman's eyes, first and foremost the annunciation of the divine energies of words, of signs and sounds that possessed a performative capacity to enact the things they represented, to participate in the evolutionary growth they signified. Only if semiosis were a progressive unfolding of the innate spirit of humanity, instead of being a channel of information open to the uses and abuses of rhetoricians and "contenders," could nineteenth-century Americans fulfill the promises afforded by both the founding Fathers and a naked continent.

Believing that the state of the language is both the index and precondition of the state of the nation, Whitman, at the time he is outlining his poetics and writing his best poetry (1855–1860), regards a poetic-linguistic revolution as the best way or at least as the necessary first step to remedy social inequality and political corruption and general alienation. In the above passage, however, which Whitman hardly touched in later editions, language (of all kinds) appears to be more a condition of than an antidote for alienation.

It is tempting to restrict Whitman's cynicism about expression to those usages that debase communication and suppress rather than arouse feeling—for example, the stale prose of scholars and academicians, the fanciful conversation of the literary salon, the stern admonishments and irksome repetitions of teachers and preachers. Obeying this temptation, one can then turn to *Leaves of Grass* and relish its corrective and refreshing vernacular utterance, rejoice in "the dialect of common sense" and "the repartee of workers" (*PW*, II, 457, 577). But whereas such recourse is invited by "Song of Myself," in "A Song of the Rolling Earth" (and many other poems from 1856 and 1860) any hope that a Whitmanian idiom might overturn the prevailing "dead" languages is foreclosed. Although Whitman directed the assertions in the above quotation toward abstract functionaries (the "singer," the "teacher," the "orator," the "actor and actress"), in the next section he turns upon himself and draws the same conclusion of impotence regarding his own expressions:

I swear I begin to see little or nothing in audible words!
I swear I think that all merges toward the presentation of the unspoken
    meanings of the earth!
Toward him who sings of the body, and of the truths of the earth,
Toward him who makes the dictionaries of the words that print cannot touch.

I swear I see what is better than to tell the best,
It is always to leave the best untold.

When I undertake to tell the best, I find I cannot,
My tongue is ineffectual on its pivots,
My breath will not be obedient to its organs,
I become a dumb man.

                                        (ll. 98–107)

Whitman becomes a "dumb man," however, not because he wants the expressive capability "to tell the best," but rather because "The best of the earth cannot be told . . ." (l. 108). It is the telling itself, not the teller, that blocks Whitman's desire. Owing to their ineradicable metaphysical seclusion beyond the poet's oracular reach, the "meanings of the earth" will not admit to representation. The supplementary action of his words prevents them from broaching the thing itself and unveiling the essential truths of man and nature (this is the Orphic poet's calling), leaving those cherished "meanings" forever "unspoken" and unprinted. As a universal presence felt individually, a ubiquitous given inaccessible to linguistic reconstruction, "the best" is too near, too enveloping, too much ourselves to yield to articulation and cognition.

To recognize and articulate "the best" would require the poet to assume a reflective distance from his "meanings," an observant position mediated by a system of reference that objectifies and thereby perverts feeling and experience. In their pure state, "the truths of the earth" elude the signifying grasp of "audible words." "[T]he common air that bathes the globe" ("Song of Myself," l. 360) disdains possession or restriction by man and his interpretations. When submitted to interpretation, "the best" loses its self-evidence, its status as "understood," and becomes the focus of debate, the subject of predications and attributions to be proved or disproved depending upon the relative persuasive force of the contestants' rhetoric. When "the best" comes to be a tool of sophistry and rhetoric, when nature, god, the soul, and the body come to be managed and directed by their representatives, democracy will have abandoned its natural foundations. Man will have traded his natural energies for their enervating proxies, while the poet, self-appointed guardian of language, will guiltily discover himself participating in the perverse substitution of words for things and signs for feelings, and furthering America's degeneration.

The only alternative is "to leave the best untold." With his realization that language fails to penetrate to the essence of things, Whitman finds himself paralyzed: "When I undertake to tell the best, I find I cannot, / My tongue is ineffectual on its pivots, / My breath will not be obedient to its organs." The Orphic mastery he had affirmed in "Song of Myself" and in his anonymous self-reviews has lapsed into a stifling impotence. The spontaneous cooperation of "tongue," "breath," "organs," and "the best" has broken down. Rather than trying to cover over this incapacitating rupture in expression or making a futile attempt to remedy it through the use of language, Whitman simply acknowledges the sign's shortcomings and reaffirms his faith in a supracontextual, extralinguistic "meaning." The fact that Whitman must employ a self-defeating medium, a fabricated language severed from its transcendental reference, necessitating interpretation, and generating more language (even a twice-removed critical metalanguage), only enhances the value and mystery of what lies beyond it and strengthens Whitman's confidence in his poetry's ability to "indicate" reality, if not "tell" it.

This confidence, however, is short-lived, and poetry is only temporarily saved from condemnation, for it is inevitable that an elevation of the inexpressible (as in "A Song of the Rolling Earth") should soon be followed by a devaluation of expression. Momentarily, Whitman finds refuge in "indication'—"Every thing indicates" ("Crossing Brooklyn Ferry," originally line 7, deleted in later editions)—as a more natural means of communicating "meaning" than print or "book-words," a deictic semiotic gesture founded upon concrete, physical action, not conventional abstraction. But nevertheless, though not as representational as printed words (loosely assuming that representation is quantifiable), "indication" still presupposes a signifying space between sign and referent and between signal and receiver.

"Indication," therefore, is prone to become skewed like any other form of expression, to waver from its destination as it is given up to desire and interpretation. In other words, putatively natural gestures such as "indication," which seemingly achieve unmediated status by virtue of their independence from the spoken and written sign, are in fact also liable to the hazards of reading. No matter how transparent or organic or symbolic the sign may be, its success still must necessarily rest upon interest, ideology, prejudice, upon the interpretive virtues and vices of willful, desirous readers.

Where is the audience, Whitman asks, who will imbibe his songs like sunshine after a spring rain? Who has withstood the terminal lessons of "the head teacher or charitable proprietor or wise statesman" ("A Song for Occupations," l. 6) and the "formulas" of "bat-eyed and materialistic priests!" ("Song of the Open Road," l. 130)? Who has remained untainted by abstract thought, analysis, interpretation? They are the fit audience for which *Leaves of Grass* was intended, but by the late 1850s Whitman has begun to doubt their existence, and hence to question his ambitions.

This is not to say that the entire career falls apart, but only that the unmitigated verve, the self-satisfaction, and the grandiose playfulness have become somewhat blunted. The public assertiveness has lost its edge, the reason for that decline lying somehow in problems of audience, publication, and review. His including positive and negative reviews of the 1855 volume in the 1856 volume may suggest continued audacity, but it also shows an increasingly anxious awareness of how others treat his work, of the crucial importance of response.

Chase writes, "In the 1856 edition of *Leaves of Grass* there is a rather nervously assertive attempt to put the house in order, to impress upon the public that the poems are intelligible and have behind them a large-scale program." After discussing Whitman's tactless marketing of Emer-

117

son's congratulatory letter, Allen tells how, for many months, "he had been 'promoting' himself as a uniquely American poet." Zweig cites his troubles with Fowler & Wells, his publishers, and says, "The 1856 edition went almost unnoticed, and apparently he was too caught up in his writings to campaign for it as he had for the first book a year before."[4] By 1857, Whitman had written dozens more poems, yet he would not find any publishing support for three more frustrating years.

Whitman makes a revealing admission along these lines in a letter dated July 28, 1857: "My immediate acquaintances, even those attached to me strongly, secretly entertain the idea that I am a great fool not to 'make something' out of my 'talents' and out of the general good will with which I am regarded. Can it be that some such notion is lately infusing itself into me also?" (*Cor*, I, 45). That is, is Whitman's self-definition succumbing to what others require him to be, what publishers, critics, enemies, and even friends define him as?

This drift of self-expression into audience-anxiety is what makes poems like "Crossing Brooklyn Ferry," according to Larson's excellent summation of this reader response issue, "a gesture, summons, or petition."[5] But although petitioning may work to some readers, to others it only poses the question of why attempt to do so. Why worry, at this point, so much about interpretation?

Because now he senses that once interpretation has begun, it gathers momentum and surreptitiously insinuates itself into human nature as a second nature (Whitman would appreciate that oxymoron), implacable in its designs and incorporating all resistances. After interpretation has vitiated the senses and the soul, every thing, every person, every feeling becomes not a presence but a sign awaiting exegesis, a ghostly demarcation of some reality we must remain insensible to. The only way to restore the divided sign to its monadic preexistence is by resorting, with greater and greater frustration and nostalgia, to yet more signs. The afflictive fact remains that "no substantive or noun, no figure or phonograph or image, stands for the beautiful mystery" (*NUPM*, I, 191).

So, if the only way to satisfy one's craving for the infinite is to rely upon the unsatisfactory finite, if the means of restoration is itself the problem, what is the poet to do? Is he to persist in his Orphic mission,

4. Chase, *Walt Whitman Reconsidered*, 99; Allen, *The Solitary Singer*, 181; Zweig, *Walt Whitman: The Making of the Poet*, 279.
5. Larson, *Whitman's Drama of Consensus*, 10.

continue to seek a language of union, compose a hundred visions and revisions in the hope of canonizing himself and America, all the while knowing that his life is a fiction? Or will he simply recall his projections, renounce his ambitions, and fade into silence and death?

This uninspiring corollary to the previous conclusion is what Whitman faces after 1856 as he begins occasionally, but with an abruptness and intensity suggesting a decisive return of the repressed, to focus his generalized critique of expression upon his own work. Now grimly conscious of the pitfalls of being read, Whitman loses confidence in words' power to bring about an unmediated experience. Regret and resentment arising from the failure of 1855 to do so takes its place. Language more and more is regarded as a catastrophe, the cause and instrument of man's expulsion from a preinterpretive golden age. Many of the best lyrics of 1860—"Out of the Cradle Endlessly Rocking," "As I Ebb'd with the Ocean of Life," "Scented Herbage of My Breast," to name a few—and parts of several other poems dwell upon this eventful "mistake" and ponder the implications it has for Whitman's career. As Whitman realizes, these poems and what inspired them tragically signal the end of the project begun five years earlier.

4
Revision

There was a crisis, say the critics. A man or woman lost, the lover forsaken and aggrieved. Poverty, the family deteriorating into disease, insanity, and pecuniary squabbling, the son dutifully assuming the role of his hated deceased father. The masterwork out of print and generally ignored, the poet reluctantly returning to hack journalism. Depressed and confused, doubting his capacity as lover, son, and poet, Whitman bleakly passed his fortieth year, he says, in a "*Slough*." Plodding along in a newspaper office, coping with family distresses (his mother's demands for money and attention, his sister's unhappy marriage, his brothers' illnesses), regretting the debasement of American ideals (he devotes much of his concern at this time to slavery, economic woes, and political corruption), Whitman was in some ways back to where he started before the first *Leaves of Grass* began to take shape in his mind.

Of course, this is not to say that *Leaves of Grass* did not transform Whitman's life. Indeed, socially, in the late 1850s, he prospered as he never had before. The trickle of admirers journeying to meet the great poet continued—some, like William Swinton, seeking professional guidance. On the steamboats and ferries, he struck up conversations that turned into enduring friendships. One recipient, quoted by Bucke, recalls how "Walt's appearance used to attract great attention from the passengers when he came on board."[1] Abby Price and her family enter-

---

1. Bucke, *Walt Whitman*, 33. For biographical accounts of these years, see Allen, *The Solitary Singer*, 207–36; Justin Kaplan, *Walt Whitman: A Life* (New York, 1980),

tained him often and introduced him to many friends and neighbors, some of whom became lifelong admirers. As editor of the Brooklyn *Daily Times*, he threw himself into social causes and reform movements. And, of most significance, he took his place in the leading bohemian circle in New York (notably Henry Clapp, Thomas Bailey Aldrich, Artemus Ward, and Ada Clare), the group meeting in Pfaff's beer cellar who made Whitman into something of a public icon. This was a far cry from the energetic but seemingly aimless Whitman of the pre–*Leaves of Grass* years. Although he had an intermittently active social life from the early 1840s onward, previous to the first publication of *Leaves of Grass* he had little access to the "in" crowds of New York culture and politics.

And yet, though his society had grown to include leading literary figures, the continuing urge to publish, the scattered references to personal disillusionment and restlessness, and his growing obsession with personal relationships indicated something inside was still unappeased. (See, for example, *NUPM*, I, 265–372, for scattered notes in which Whitman continues to forecast what great poetry should be, to give advice to himself, and to question what he has done.) Something unusual had *not* happened to him personally after he had published his verses. It now seemed that whereas in the early 1850s, Whitman could look forward to a literary event both founding an American idiom and promising him not only a new identity but also a catalytic role in American history, in the late 1850s he could only look backward to that event as a spectacular but all too brief moment of discovery and creativity, one whose effect seemed puny in light of his outsized ambitions. The present he experienced as a rather unexciting aftermath to his cataclysmic emergence into world culture, his belated rebirth as the American Orpheus. All the old personal, and national, problems lingered, and his psychological conflicts and sexual ambivalences increased.

For Whitman, it is clear that, save perhaps for his hospital work, writing was the least threatening way to cope with his crises or sublimate his frustrations. Certainly, *Calamus* (*calamus*, "reed," "quill pen") and *Enfans d'Adam* are contrasting attempts to overcome sexual tensions, "The Eighteenth Presidency!" a necessary expression of political outrage, *Drum-Taps* a gentle rendering of his introduction to wartime conditions.

232–40; Chase, *Walt Whitman: Reconsidered*, 111–27; Black, *Whitman's Journeys into Chaos*, 171–87; and Zweig, *Walt Whitman: The Making of the Poet*, 276–325.

Poring over the thousands of pages of diaries, notebooks, jottings, and observations on scraps of paper (most of which he retained), drafts of poems and essays, letters, bills, and so on, not to mention the published works, one realizes how much Whitman relied on writing for succor and reassurance, even therapy. Apart from the massive amount of texts covering subjects as diverse as ethnic history, medicine, local politics, real estate, and pedagogy, there is a tremendous body of writing about himself: autobiographical notes and narratives, self-directed advice, defenses and self-reviews not yet disguised by a friend's signature, data on financial transactions (extensive enough to be pathological), and enigmatic half-disclosures of private feelings and doings. That so many of his self-accounts and descriptions are fictionalized only supports the idea that writing was a strategy, a means for Whitman to dispel influences and occurrences, both internal and external, that threatened the self-image he needed to construct.

In terms of Whitman's poetics, however, writing is not strategic, for the self is not a construction and language is not its raw material. Instead, the self is body and soul, a "solid personality, with blood and brawn" (*PW*, II, 385), a natural, biological being presently submerged under social constructions alien to it. And language, in the mouth of the American poet, is the salutary instrument that tears down those artificial restraints, exposes the factitiousness of everything that stands in the way of personal freedom, liberates the self from deadening cultural go-betweens, and unifies it with other selves.

The question, then, posed to the poet in 1855 is, given his intuitive self-certainty and self-confidence, what language, what idiom, what manner of speaking best publicizes that self and remains true to feeling? What poetic medium eschews tradition and authority and rejuvenates the self? What order of signs is guided solely by those desires and impulses arising spontaneously from within? If Whitman is able to canonize such a language, Americans will finally live according to their "fullest poetical nature" (*PW*, II, 434) and "tally" the scope and majesty of the continent they inhabit. Constituted by Whitman and bequeathed to others simply and straightforwardly, this natural, democratic vernacular harmonious with human feeling would revivify the "visionary compact" bonding New World peoples together. It would reunite immigrant and native, capitalist and laborer, sons and fathers, man and wife (relations that Whitman, growing up in a divisive family in mid-century

Brooklyn, personally saw breaking apart), and "help the forming of a great aggregate Nation" (*PW*, II, 726).

Leaves of Grass, 1855, was to fulfill Whitman's visionary projection; but, as we have seen, the diversity and seeming arbitrariness of reader responses following its publication revealed the necessity not only of the poet's wielding a natural language but also of his cultivating "natural reading." Many poems of 1856 try to do just this, to circumvent any improper receptions or critical exegeses that hinder the liberating-unifying process initiated when Whitman begins composing "Song of Myself." That is, the 1856 lyrics proclaim an empathic form of reading as the just, congenial, and effective way to experience literature, as opposed to reading characterized by aesthetic distance and a predisposition for critical judgment. Hence, the threat of misinterpretation is displaced from author to reader. Those who react to *Leaves of Grass* with appropriate sensitivity and feeling are applauded as natural compatriots. Those who react with invective or even excessive discernment are counseled, "Reread the poems—open yourself to feeling—respond with your heart, not your intellect."

Tracing this perhaps simplistic (Whitman also simplifies events in his autobiographical writings) but generally accurate narrative of the progress of Whitman's poetic ambitions and fears on through the 1860 edition, we find, however, at crucial moments, something of a reversal of the previous conclusion. That is, in a masochistic reaction to his situation in the late 1850s, Whitman comes occasionally to portray himself as a misconceived failure and denounces himself in devastating terms precisely the antithesis of those he used to celebrate himself. Periodically, even in the sanguine, soaring, visionary poems, Whitman begins to deprecate his own utterances for their inadequacy, "arrogance," or ineffectiveness. He begins to write lines denigrating his poetry: "The words of my mouth, rude, ignorant, arrogant—my many faults and derelictions" ("As the Time Draws Nigh," originally line 14, later deleted); "I am indifferent to my own songs" ("Long I Thought That Knowledge Alone Would Suffice," l. 10; this poem appeared only in the 1860 edition).

And in "Myself and Mine," he writes:

(Who are you? you mean devil? And what are you secretly guilty of, all
    your life?
Will you turn aside all your life? Will you grub and chatter all your life?

123

And who are you—blabbing by rote, years, pages, languages, reminiscences,
Unwitting to-day that you do not know how to speak a single word?)

(ll. 14–17)

The questions in the first line echo similar blatant rhetorical questions
such as those found in "Song of Myself": "What blurt is it about virtue
and about vice?" (l. 464); "Shall I pray? Shall I venerate and be cere-
monious?" (l. 398); "Do you take it I would astonish?" (l. 384); "Do I
contradict myself?" (l. 1325); "Have you felt so proud to get at the
meaning of poems?" (l. 32). Here, Whitman half-mockingly challenges
conventional interpretations of him and his works and then inverts the
values attached to those judgments or simply asserts that they do not
apply. But in this passage, Whitman directs the questions to himself.
Unlike the brash openings in "Song of Myself," they point an accusing
finger at the poet and then disallow any justification for his "secret"
guilt. In the earlier poem, the argument following each question saved
him from censure by showing the question's impertinence, but now any
further statement has no power to do so.

Indeed, writing and arguing are seen to be prominent reasons for his
guilt. Instead of facing squarely the things themselves and "endowing
them with the glows and glories and final illustriousness which belongs
to every real thing, and to real things only" (*PW*, II, 716), Whitman
"turns aside" to "grub and chatter," and displaces "the real reality"
("Scented Herbage of My Breast," l. 33) with his own immaterial phrases.
Instead of originating poetry through spontaneous ejaculatory utterance,
he "blabs by rote, years, pages, languages, reminiscences," his creative
inspiration degenerating into mechanical, "parrot-like repetitions" (*PW*,
II, 736). Incapable of meeting his own requirements, "unwitting" and
ignorant of "how to speak a single word," Whitman undoes his poetic
identity and demands a new answer to the contempt-filled question,
Who are you? He cannot say nor can anyone else: "I charge you, too,
forever, reject those who would expound me—for I cannot expound myself" ("Myself and Mine," l. 27).

If Whitman does not know "how to speak," who does? If it is true that
the "language experiment" has failed to produce results—"in libraries
I lie as one dumb, a gawk, or unborn or dead" ("Whoever You Are Holding Me Now in Hand," l. 16)—and Whitman must renounce his earlier
poetry—"My songs cease—I abandon them" ("So Long," l. 51)—what

is to take its place? If the language of *Leaves of Grass*—the language intended to resurrect the primal energy of words and bring the "living speech in the real world" (*DN*, III, 735) into literature—collapses under the poet's critical rereading, then can any language retain its natural characteristics once it has been articulated, not to mention versified and published? What poet and what language can escape the accusations Whitman levels against himself and his poems? Who can live up to his requirements for poetry (that it be natural, organic, kinetic) and embody his description of the poet (that he be spontaneous, magnetic, Orphic, original)? How can one balance the oppositions Whitman uses to define the poet's task as, for example, he does in a relatively plain decree in *Democratic Vistas*?

Observing, rapport, and with intuition, the shows and forms presented by Nature, the sensuous luxuriance, the beautiful in living men and women, the actual play of passions, in history and life—above all, from those developments either in Nature or human personality in which power, (dearest of all to the sense of the artist,) transacts itself—out of these, and seizing what is in them, the poet, the esthetic worker in any field, by the divine magic of his genius, projects them, their analogies, by curious removes, indirections, in literature and art. (No useless attempt to repeat the material creation, by daguerreotyping the exact likeness by mortal mental means.) (*PW*, II, 419)

The poet is to "observe" but not interpret, to "project" but not repeat, to endow but not add to. Although the poet must take "Nature" and "human personality" as his subject matter, in transcribing them (with "intuition") he must leave them pure and intact. Without "turning aside" from the "shows and forms presented by Nature" and "the actual play of passions," the "esthetic worker" must operate by "curious removes" and "indirections," ever respectful of the integrity and self-sufficiency of that which he represents.

In this way, the poet escapes "useless attempts to repeat the material creation," finding photographic or journalistic re-creations of quotidian life limited and uninspiring. Although the "mortal mental means" of writing poetry provides realistic copies of physical nature and enumerates without distortion natural facts and details (granting such "daguerreotyping" is possible), it ignores nature's spiritual dimension, its values and truths and morals that somehow reflect the "deepest basic elements and loftiest final meanings, of history and man" (*PW*, II, 425). Remaining at the level of "the sensible universe," this mere cameralike realism "do[es] not tend to ideas" nor does it "feed the highest mind, the soul." Only by negating the material world "does a human being, his spirit, ascend above, and justify, objective Nature" (419).

But those who try to achieve transcendence and probe the profounder meanings of existence run the risk of straying from nature and supplanting the sanctioned order of things with their own willful, idiosyncratic wishes. What is to prevent "the divine magic of his genius" from perverting an accurate representation of the world, or from arbitrarily imposing, however unintentionally, its own acquisitive desires upon the Logos? And even if the poet's desires concur with nature, the next and most fundamental problem is how he is to erase the supplementary effects of his medium? Pushing his words into the essence of reality, will those words not restructure reality according to their own grammar, their own "curious removes" and tropic "indirections"?

These fears appeared in 1855 and 1856 to be merely provisional obstacles to genuine communication, stylistic or interpretive errors corrected by a new "personality" exerting a new idiom. But by 1860, Whitman's fears have become certainties—the pitfalls of writing he now believes are inescapable: "Which is the poem, or any book, that is not diseased?" (*NUPM*, I, 373; written probably in the late 1850s). Looking back over his own poetry, he comes to distrust his "rapport" and "intuition" (with and of nature and humanity) and to despair over the feasibility of writing nature or himself veraciously and transparently, of using language to represent with clarity and surety the principles of existence and the truths of the soul. The regulations Whitman sets forth in *Democratic Vistas* he admits in his poetry are impossible to follow: there is no way to observe without interpreting, to project without repeating, to endow without adding to, to transcribe without de-forming and re-forming.

Composition, whether conceived mimetically or expressively, means translation, substituting a technical practice loaded with quotation, dead metaphors, standardized rhythms, and perfunctory phrases, for either the tangible book of nature or the inarticulate language of the heart. Initially, Whitman believed he could guard against tradition and convention and other preexistent man-made forms alien to original inspiration and actual things by "eluding those highly refined imported and gilt-edged themes, and sentimental and butterfly flights, pleasant to orthodox pub-

lishers" (*PW*, II, 412). If Whitman, by "becom[ing] a candid and un-
loosed summer-poet" ("So Long!" originally line 4, later deleted), could
inject invention and freedom and individualism and "athleticism" into
poetic practice, the customary forms and styles would be exposed as obsolete, timeworn usages no longer responsive to human feeling.

But in the wake of *Leaves of Grass*, a new race of poets and a new vein
of poetry has, in Whitman's own announcement, not followed: "Never
was anything more wanted than, to-day, and here in the States, the poet
of the modern is wanted, or the great literatus of the modern" (*PW*, II,
365). Although Whitman sometimes blames the postwar sociopolitical
situation for the dearth of great literature in the 1860s, 1870s, and 1880s
(relative to the decade preceding the war), in many poems of 1860 he
accuses his own poetry of insufficiently answering America's call for an
indigenous, instigating literary idiom. He usually phrases his self-
critique in terms more personal than political, but the implication that he
has disappointed his own nationalistic mandate ensues closely upon his
deprecation of earlier poems. Hence, in his own opinion, he has satisfied
neither the individual goal of self-expression nor the social goal of literary reform.

Such a conclusion may surprise casual readers of Whitman accus-
tomed to the sanguine poems glorifying the self, the soul, the Union,
America, humanity, nature, and so on. Whitman's ambition to embrace
and be embraced by his culture carried him through several idealistic,
inspirational poems (as well as some embarrassingly bathetic ones). His
mood is usually profoundly utopian and optimistic even in the face of
death and suffering, making the occasions of bitter despair seem anomalous (though his optimism seems to be rarely unaccompanied by some
kind of despair). One might say that the combined moments of self-
detraction and criticism of previous writings comprise only one motif
among many others in the 1860 edition, and it may be objected that sin-
gling it out as the most significant motif reveals more about the critic's
predispositions than it does the actual state of affairs in the poetry. Other
themes equally prevalent in 1860 and deserving readers' attention are
Whitman's bold yet "furtive" homoeroticism (mainly in *Calamus*) and
his visionary notion of democracy (mainly in the *Chants Democratic*
section). Surely the latter themes disclose more of the poet's ideas and
intentions than does his faultfinding attitude toward earlier poems.

But the poet's ideas and intentions are not identical with his poems, which, as translations, necessarily effect a distortion upon their "primary" material, immediate experience, and then try to conceal that distortion. (As we shall see, this is precisely why Whitman finds fault with them!) And notwithstanding Whitman's express desire to "make a song of the organic bargains of These States" and "sing the song of companionship" ("Starting from Paumanok," ll. 74 and 86), it is remarkable how often issues or problems of expression and language come into play in poems overtly concerned with politics or sexuality. For example, when Whitman says in "Our Old Feuillage" (originally "Chants Democratic 4"), "how can I do less than pass the clew of the union of them, to afford the like to you? / Whoever you are! how can I but offer you divine leaves, that you also be eligible as I am?" (ll. 80–81), he suggests that participation in the physical and spiritual "continent of Democracy" (l. 9) begins with one's receiving "the clew of the union," the "word en masse" delivered by the bard. That is, the utopian brotherhood of American citizens begins with their mutual recognition of a communal sign and its emotive import.

In "Scented Herbage of My Breast" (originally "Calamus 2"), on the other hand, language—or at least his own past words—seems to impede Whitman from giving the "clew" of "adhesiveness": "Come, I am determined to unbare this broad breast of mine—I have long enough stifled and choked; / Emblematic and capricious blades, I leave you—now you serve me not, / Away! I will say what I have to say, by itself, / I will escape from the sham that was proposed to me, / I will sound myself and comrades only" (ll. 21–24). Likewise, in "A Glimpse," Whitman notes the gratuitousness of words during a genuine exchange of feeling: "There we two, content, happy in being together, speaking little, perhaps not a word" (l. 5). Further, when immersed in healthy "masculine" contact, Whitman finds words to be superfluous and intrusive: "When he whom I love travels with me, or sits a long while holding me by the hand, / When the subtle air, the impalpable, the sense that words and reason hold not, surround us and pervade us, / Then I am charged with untold and untellable wisdom—I am silent, I require nothing further" ("Of the Terrible Doubt of Appearances," ll. 11–13).

And yet, in other *Calamus* poems, Whitman claims that writing is beneficial and, for him, somewhat obligatory. He answers the opening question of Calamus 32 (the question is the poem's later title), "What think you I take my pen in hand to record?" with "I record of two simple men I saw to-day on the pier, in the midst of the crowd, parting the part-ing of dear friends" (ll. 1 and 5). In other words, Whitman writes to "celebrate the need of comrades" ("In Paths Untrodden," l. 18), to "re-cord" and preserve and understand "manly attachment" (l. 12) despite the fact that such "Calamus feelings" transcend words. Verbalizing those feelings and experiences makes them more acceptable and tractable, al-lowing Whitman a momentary cathartic relief for the anguish and self-loathing he suffers for his homoerotic desires (feelings divulged most tellingly by the *Calamus* group and by some of the more importunate letters to Peter Doyle, Lewis Brown, Harry Stafford, and other young "lovers" over the years). Even though "adhesiveness" exists "Not in sounded and resounded words—chattering words, echoes, dead words" ("Not Heaving from My Ribb'd Breast Only," l. 12), vocalizing "ad-hesiveness," substituting a social proclamation of homoeroticism for its mute, private, "physiological" manifestations, nevertheless provides Whitman with a certain satisfaction and appeasement, a vicarious enjoy-ment of a desire he is uncomfortable with.[2]

Whitman accurately condenses this contradictory relation between words and desire or feeling in one of the last of the *Calamus* poems, "Here the Frailest Leaves of Me": "Here I shade down and hide my thoughts—I do not myself expose them, / And yet they expose me more than all my other poems" (ll. 2–3). Words both "hide" and "expose" his "thoughts" simultaneously. They represent, both reveal and conceal, his desires in an aporetic movement exemplifying what Whitman calls "the divine law of indirections" ("Laws for Creations," l. 5), what contemporary 1850s Hegelianism would term "mediation" (on the assumption that the middle term is necessary but only provisional, something to be sublated) and what modern criticism might term "figuration" or "differance" (with the middle term resisting being dialectically overcome).

As this summary statement (and several other lines found in 1860 ad-ditions, many of which I have been noting and explicating) makes clear, Whitman is ever acutely conscious of the implications and effects of "in-direction," even in poems ostensibly about homoeroticism or utopian politics or any other Whitmanian theme. That Whitman continues to raise questions regarding his signs—as "indirect," are they still trans-parent, natural, adequate, and faithful to their source, or are they opaque,

2. See Kaplan, *Walt Whitman: A Life*, 245.

artificial, alien to, and diverging from their source?—especially when he apparently is trying to be absolutely sincere, suggests that expression is the most fundamental, though not the only, issue confronting the poet attempting to write a purely limpid poetry and the critic attempting an interpretation of it. For the critic, it is the will to truth that is at stake, the tireless endeavor to penetrate the text and uncover its animating core. But for Whitman, it is his will itself that is at stake, the universal narcissistic desire to make words and objects conform to feeling and satisfy the dis-ease that prompted desire in the "first" place.

That desire reaches an impasse by 1860. The single event subverting Whitman's faith in having inaugurated a living vernacular consonant with feeling is, in short, becoming a reader of his own poems. Though it sounds innocent enough, rereading his own poems four or five years after their initial composition is, in fact, the most devastating occurrence in Whitman's poetic career. What happens is that, during the late 1850s and early in 1860, especially after he receives word from Thayer & Eldridge (in February) that they wish to publish a third edition, Whitman not only composes dozens of new poems but also begins to revise previously published material, changing titles, altering punctuation, adding stanza numbers, and rearranging the order of poems, as well as "correcting" specific lines and phrases. The question to be asked is, Why should a language of the heart require modification? Whitman insisted that the Deathbed Edition should "absolutely supersede all previous ones" (*Cor,* V, 275) and that it should contain "always an unmistakable, deep down, unobliterable division line" marking off "the book complete as [he] left it" and "whatever may be added to [it]" (*LGCRE,* 575). But why did it require thirty-seven years of editing before it was finished? Why should Whitman, in the late 1850s, begin to treat his poems as inconsistent with their emotive birth, even going so far as to ask Hector Tyndale for advice as to "where [he] could be bettered in [his] poems" and to ask Fitz-James O'Brien how the poems are *"lacking"* (*NUPM,* I, 351).

The answer is in the question itself, in the simple fact that Whitman must make a judgment, that he feels compelled to clarify, define, interpret the discourse that supposedly rendered interpretation unnecessary. That is to say, as he rereads *Leaves of Grass,* 1855 and 1856, and finds himself engaged in an interpretive revisionary procedure, Whitman inevitably becomes the very reader he guarded himself against earlier!

When he tells himself, "In future *Leaves of Grass. Be More severe* with the final revisions of the poem" (*NUPM*, I, 385; dated late 1850s), he contradicts his Orphic intentions. Instead of adopting the receptive, intuitive attitude he valorizes as the ideal reading posture, the sole manner of adhering to the spirit of *Leaves of Grass*, Whitman evaluates and analyzes and revises his poems (ostensibly to improve them), thus to an extent exemplifying the trenchant, caviling modes of criticism he despises and fears.

As an active reader submitting the text to examination, Whitman unconsciously marks the distance between himself and his expression. Experiencing no immediate intuitive apprehension of what should be a self-evincing idiom (which would preclude interpretation, especially on the part of the one who originated that language), Whitman now feels estranged from his creations. Like any other reader who must approach the poem as someone else's quotation, he must postulate the "Personality" lurking behind the words in order to reexperience the initial inspiration. In doing so, Whitman consigns his "poems of futurity" to the past, reduces them to brief manifestations of feeling that can be restored to their primary organic magnetism only by a tenuous retrospective interpretive reconstruction. Having to re-cognize his own willfully objectified, printed self, Whitman suddenly and astonishingly realizes the impracticality of his fundamental poetic ambition—to incarnate the soul in the word.

Nowhere is Whitman's devastating insight, his newfound consciousness of the "failure" of language and the inevitability of interpretation, more concentrated and poignant than it is in "As I Ebb'd with the Ocean of Life." Although his notebooks and diaries contain much self-criticism in regards to health and to personal relationships, they betray hardly any self-deprecation in regards to his writing (one clear exception being "The real truth is no doubt infinitely beyond all these little broken and jagged hints," *NUPM*, I, 446). And the rest of the poetry (apart from "As I Ebb'd" and the more painful 1860 lyrics I have been discussing) rarely sustains any serious doubt or cynicism beyond a few phrases or lines, moments usually relieved by the resuscitating powers of the soul or of nature. But the seemingly anomalous character of "As I Ebb'd" has not prevented Whitman scholars, particularly those taking a psycho-biographical approach, from emphasizing its poetic excellence and its centrality in the

Whitman corpus (Harold Bloom calls it "the most moving of all Whitman's poems.")[3]

Whitman himself indicated the poem's importance in 1860 by placing it first in the *Leaves of Grass* cluster, then again in 1881, when he rearranged the poems into new clusters, by setting it just after "Out of the Cradle Endlessly Rocking" in the *Sea-Drift* grouping. But notwithstanding Whitman's care in positioning the poem and criticism's extensive probing of it, nobody has yet interpreted "As I Ebb'd" strictly within the framework of Whitman's poetics, to situate it within the context opened by Whitman's struggle to align signs and composition and reading with nature.

An interpretation of "As I Ebb'd" based upon the categories and concepts structuring his poetics seems to be called for from the opening lines: "Elemental drifts! / O I wish I could impress others as you and the waves have just been impressing me" (lines later deleted).[4] Again, as in Section 25 of "Song of Myself," Whitman proposes to himself the primary Orphic directive—to answer nature's satiating forms and exhilarating forces with an equally gratifying and "impressive" organic upsurge of feeling. If Whitman's "Sea-Drifts" prove to be as affective and beautiful and plain as the "Elemental drifts" comprising the natural world, if he can discover in himself the same innervating processes and emanations that nature possesses, then not only will his bardic task be completed but also his private *"Slough"* and despair will not seem so isolating and irrational.

This is why Whitman in the succeeding lines begins to scan the seascape for sights and sounds that might objectify his emotions, to enumerate the "Chaff, straw, splinters of wood, weeds, and the sea-gluten, / Scum, scales from shining rocks, leaves of salt-lettuce, left by the tide"

---

3. For readings of "As I Ebb'd," see Chase, *Walt Whitman: Reconsidered,* 124–27; Miller, *Walt Whitman's Poetry,* 44–47; Black, *Whitman's Journeys into Chaos,* 55–61; Harold Bloom, *A Map of Misreading* (New York, 1975), 178–83; Zweig, *Walt Whitman: The Making of the Poet,* 307–12; and Larson, *Whitman's Drama of Consensus,* 199–204.

4. Over the years, Whitman made several changes to the poem. Initially, it had stanza numbers (1–16) and no title. Section numbers and the title "Elemental Drifts" were added in 1867. In 1881, stanza numbers were dropped, and the poem received its final title. Each successive edition saw more and more lines and phrases trimmed away, many of which I use to support my argument.

(ll. 11–12), in the hope that they offer some justification or at least some consolation for his "ebbing" life. As he modestly puts it, "I thought the old thought of likenesses" (l. 14)—not to exemplify the Transcendental doctrine of correspondence, but rather to secure a reassuring narcissistic identification of the soul's moods with nature:

> These [likenesses] you presented to me, you fish-shaped island,
> As I wended the shores I know,
> As I walked with that eternal self of me, seeking types.
>
> (ll. 15–17; "eternal" here and in line 7
> was later changed to "electric.")

Another name for "seeking types" is reading (no pun intended). Not Quaker religious types and not Wordsworthian "types and symbols of eternity," but rather "types" of his own sole self, the fragments and waste and debris scattered along the shoreline, discarded by the "fierce old mother" (l. 52), the sea, but now sympathetically drawing his attention. He is "seized by the spirit that trails in the lines underfoot, / In the rim, the sediment, that stands for all the water and all the land of the globe" (ll. 8–9). Whereas earlier the poet sang "the song of me rising from bed and meeting the sun" ("Song of Myself," l. 29) or wandered along "singing in the west, . . . strik[ing] up for a new world" ("Starting from Paumanok," l. 14), now it is the disused "sediment" and neglected "castaways" that he finds adaptable to his vision.

The next stanza extends Whitman's identification with "those slender winrows" and completely deflates the bard's cosmic pretensions. He abruptly shifts to the present tense and describes the shores he "knows *not*," thereby making a personal division between his past and present, knowledge and ignorance, inspiration and suffocation:

> As I wend the shores I know not,
> As I listen to the dirge, the voices of men and women wrecked,
> As I inhale the impalpable breezes that set in upon me,
> As the ocean so mysterious rolls toward me closer and closer,
> At once I find, the least thing that belongs to me, or that I see or touch,
>   I know not;

I, too, but signify, at the utmost, a little washed-up drift,
A few sands and dead leaves to gather,
Gather, and merge myself as part of the sands and drift.

(ll. 18–24; the fifth line was later deleted.)

In the ocean's funereal music, in the seaside muse's "impalpable breezes" (which bring on depression, not exultation), in the "little washed-up drift" sprinkled haphazardly on the beach, Whitman has found his "meaning," his highest "signification." As a "drift," he is part of nature but also haplessly subject to natural forces beyond his ken and control (the verbs "listen," "inhale," "held," and "seized" in the previous stanza all have a passive connotation). Being a natural thing does not mitigate his sense of alienation or impotence: "the least thing that belongs to me, or that I see or touch, I know not." His prior self-characterization as a "kosmos" ("Song of Myself," l. 497) and "a growth and idiom of America" (*In Re*, 23) now sounds like absurd hubris, a vain delusion no longer inoffensive by being consciously comic or at least only half-serious. Offering no mitigating context for these lines (a context that might reduce these self-admonishments to a rhetorical stance), "As I Ebb'd" is Whitman's sad retreat from the bardic expansiveness of "Song of Myself."

However, the bardic self is not the only privileged thing undone in this poem. Because they were to be frank extensions of his own unique identity and to confirm his seminal place in American history by ushering in an emotive idiom to abet the progressive liberation of mankind, Whitman's poems must share the poet's fate. Whitman realizes this only too well, for he now regards his poems as "A few sands and dead leaves to gather." The divine leaves of grass, in "Song of Myself" "no less than the journeywork of the stars" (l. 663), have now become wayward "dead leaves" tossed upon the comfortless shoreline at random. The "songs of the rolling earth" have eroded into "A few sands," a deterioration made explicit by the imperial "real Me" in the next verse paragraph: "Pointing in silence to all these songs, and then to the sand beneath" (l. 31, added in 1867). (The latter analogy is prefigured by the phrase "lines underfoot" in line 8, which refers not only to the crooked borderlines made in the sand by the receding waves but also to lines of verse, to words arranged in metrical feet.) With his profoundest achievements lumped together as miniscule, insignificant grains of sand or inert, extinct leaves banished from the "ocean of life," with what resources is Whitman (and how is the appreciative critic, for that matter) to respond to such peremptorily reductive comparisons?

With typical Whitmanian abandon, the poet turns his self-recriminations to poetic use and magnifies melodramatically his songs' shortcomings, even going so far as to distinguish his poetry as the major cause of his present shame and despair. Notwithstanding the many personal misfortunes Whitman suffered in the late 1850s (the dearth of critical praise for *Leaves of Grass* from 1857 to 1860, the death of his father a week after the first edition was published, poverty and illness in the rest of the Whitman family) and the national evils he saw coming to a head during the same period (slavery, economic privation, the decline of American statesmanship into party politics and the spoils system), both of which were in a way solved for Whitman by the war, in the following passage it is his poetry, not his or his country's "life," that disheartens him:

O baffled, balked, bent to the very earth, here preceding what follows,
Oppressed with myself that I have dared to open my mouth,
Aware now, that, amid, all the blab whose echoes recoil upon me, I have not
    once had the least idea who or what I am,
But that before all my insolent poems the real Me still stands untouched,
    untold, altogether unreached,
Withdrawn far, mocking me with mock-congratulatory signs and bows,
With peals of distant ironical laughter at every word I have written or
    shall write,
Striking me with insults till I fall helpless upon the sand.
                    (ll. 25–31; the last line was deleted in
                    1867 and the line noted above, "Pointing
                    in silence . . ." was substituted for it.)

To understand these bitter, affecting lines in the context of Whitman's poetry and thought, we must recall the function words (not just poetic language) ideally are to serve in his poetics. That is, they should act as transparent presentations of feeling, live organic embodiments of the soul's passions. They should evince the "real Me" to other souls awakened to freedom and "happiness," not portray a "false Me" in traditional literary clichés to intellects caught up in "criticism." The word's success depends upon its dissolution while it simultaneously manifests the soul (or the psyche, pneuma, spirit, and so on—all extrinsic names, to Whitman, of the same extralinguistic emotive presence motivating all human behavior). If the word fails to dissolve and instead maintains its resistance, its material priority over the ineffable spirit underlying it, then the poet has merely furthered the insulation of individuals, their entrapment within a curtain of signs. And not only has he placed a linguistic barrier between himself and others but also between that empirical part of himself that engages with the world and the "Me myself" standing "Apart from the pulling and hauling" ("Song of Myself," l. 75).

These nonhuman inter- and intrasubjective divisions are precisely what Whitman here accuses himself of advancing. Because the "real Me" remains supremely intact—indeed, profoundly imperturbable—because Whitman mystifies it by setting it beyond signification, any further attempt to represent it is doomed to fail. The fault, however, is due less to any poetic incapacity than it is to the linguistic dilemma the poet faces. The attack is not so much on the poet-agent as it is on the means Whitman must necessarily use to represent the "real Me." Of course, to become the "outsetting bard" and "authorize" the "real Me," Whitman must resort to the word, the printed, stabilized, spatialized, encoded sign. But the word refuses to vanish in the face of a self struggling for recognition; it jealously veils the "Me" it stands for and frustrates Whitman's initial claims for his poetry.

As the word is not the point Whitman wishes his poems to settle on, he can only lament his inevitable mistake and question his life's work. Because of one fateful, ill-conceived decision—he "dared to open [his] mouth"—Whitman now indulges in a brutal self-criticism. The violent verbs ("baffled," "balked," "bent," "oppressed," "recoil") whose object is the poet convey the bitter regret he feels at having attempted to write an "expression . . . transcendent and new" (*PW*, II, 437), to celebrate himself in "a poetry with cosmic and dynamic features of magnitude and limitlessness suitable to the human soul" (*PW*, II, 718). Although he intended his poems to exalt his individuality, they now seem to lack any "cosmic and dynamic features." Having none of the soul's "transcendent" qualities, they now "recoil upon" him and certify his ignorance of self. What began as a journey of self-discovery in "Song of Myself" now ends with Whitman lost "amid all the blab," divorced from the emotive truth concealed behind an impenetrable wall of signs. The poems that make up this wall Whitman musters together with the indiscriminate adjective "all," suggesting that the problem lay not in this or that poem but in the overall design, in the poetics out of which the poems sprang. That Whitman ever thought his poems could embody a self or transmit feeling without transforming the latter causes him to judge them as "insolent."

Language appears as a seducer and betrayer, a spurious talking cure luring him into a false sense of integration and reconciliation and self-knowledge. Just as Freud progressively realized that verbal catharsis offers only temporary appeasement of anxiety (that is, it addresses a symptom without revealing the underlying problem, perhaps because verbalization constitutes the problem as underlying), so Whitman realizes that individual poems have no enduring power to heal or even to express what he feels inside. Indeed, the fact that they do endure in print long after the feeling has subsided only aggravates Whitman's frustration, for when he returns to them for re-cognition, he feels doubly estranged and twice-removed: instead of helping Whitman to "close" with his soul or the "real Me," language has separated and come between them. Hence, with unanswerable superiority, the "real Me" ridicules Whitman's pitifully inadequate "songs" with nonverbal derision. The taunts assume the form of "mock-congratulatory signs and bows," "distant ironical laughter," and an incontrovertible "Pointing in silence."

Because language is the reason for Whitman's culpability, and thus is itself the disease it purports to cure, how is the poet to answer the "real Me's" charges? Once again, Whitman entirely relinquishes himself to them. In his resentment, he repudiates altogether any permanent knowledge or satisfaction to be derived from poetry:

O I perceive I have not understood anything—not a single object—and that no
    man ever can.
I perceive Nature here in sight of the sea, is taking advantage of me, to dart
    upon me, and sting me,
Because I was assuming so much,
And because I have dared to open my mouth to sing at all.
                (ll. 32–34; the third line was deleted in 1867.)

Because his words could not adequately contain the feeling that occasioned them, Whitman's initial and unqualified optimism ("I was assuming so much") collapses into an all-encompassing skepticism. He feels "taken advantage of," exposed as insignificant and presumptuous, revealed in all his trivial facticity by a recondite force surpassing the verbal skills of the proud poet. Nature exercises its retribution on him like an unseen, irritating insect—"to dart upon me, and sting me"—torturing Whitman for his assumed superiority, his pretensions that he could translate the meanings of nature (for example, the bird's song in "Out of the Cradle Endlessly Rocking") without subjugating or impoverishing nature with his own exiguous meanings and defective words.

His failure to express the inexpressible compels Whitman to take refuge in a blank denial of any expression, especially that which would represent a transcendent or extralinguistic origin, be it "Nature" or the "real Me." Caught between these two polar antagonists, he can "perceive" only the meager limits of his understanding, the "pasteboard masks" language holds up to him. This harsh and unredemptive knowledge of ignorance offers him no consolation, for though it inspires him to write a moving, eloquent dejection ode, he nevertheless feels hapless and impotent, a shrunken relic of the bardic giant he "projected" in earlier writings.

Whitman's assumption of a regressive ignorance is accompanied in the rest of the poem by a fantasized return an infantile relationship with his parents: "Paumanok," his father, and the "ocean of life," his mother.[5] But what he asks for them is not simply a kind of primal, inarticulate, womblike love and security. Throwing himself down on the sand ("your breast, my father"), he says, "Breathe to me, while I hold you close, the secret of the wondrous murmuring I envy, / For I fear I shall become crazed, if I cannot emulate it, and utter myself as well as it" (l. 50; the second line was dropped in 1867). Whitman implores his father to inspire him ("Breathe to me") with the hermetic "meanings" of nature ("the secret of the wondrous murmuring"), to empower him with the same expressive strength exhibited by the waves and clouds and "that sobbing dirge of Nature" (l. 67) so that he may "emulate [both rival and imitate] it, and utter [him]self as well as it." The Oedipal ambivalences are obvious, but what sets this passage apart is the linking of his father, or a paternal *imago*, with the occult, meaningful side of nature, the very "content" he needs desperately to capture in his poems.

5. For a reading of how the geography in the poem operates as parental images, see Miller, *Walt Whitman's Poetry*, 44–47. See Black, *Whitman's Journeys into Chaos*, 58, for a Freudian reading of Whitman's allegorizing of his parents.

As we have seen, Whitman had previously cast nature as a stern preceptor threatening the poet with annihilation if he fails to "tally" nature faithfully, but he never gave to nature a paternal aspect. After reading this section of "As I Ebb'd," its elision of the family romance and poetic inspiration, one senses in the scenes of instruction and foreboding in previous poems the displaced fears and unfulfillments of childhood. This is borne out by the soothing discharge effect this sudden return and acceptance of the repressed has on Whitman. In the next lines, he declares, "Sea-raff! Crook-tongued waves! / O, I will yet sing, some day, what you have said to me" (lines deleted in 1867). Acknowledging his father's power and his own craving for paternal love, Whitman no longer rejects any presumed weaknesses and shortcomings, those parts of himself that fall short of his ego ideal. He can now say of himself, "I too am but a trail of drift and debris" (l. 43), and say to his mother (whom he usually idealizes but who most likely disapproved of any closeness between young Walter and his father), "Rustle not up so hoarse and angry against my feet, as I touch you, or gather from you. / I mean tenderly by you" (ll. 54–55). Intimacy with father in no way threatens intimacy with mother. This is Whitman's final, conscious renegotiation of the unconscious Oedipal contract that has failed him for forty years.

Not only can he admit his paltry existence and request equally from his parents the unconditional love he deserved as a child, but also, and perhaps of most importance at this stage of his life and career, Whitman can acquiesce in his own personal death: "See! from my dead lips the ooze exuding at last!" (l. 59). This ghastly image recalls several graphic death scenes portrayed in many of the puerile short stories Whitman wrote back in the 1840s, scenes generally involving a brutal, withdrawn father (or a paternal substitute) and/or a clinging, ineffective mother.[6]

But whereas Whitman's juvenilia remain at the level of trite sentimentalism and the culminating death scenes serve merely to express familial resentment, the corpse image in "As I Ebb'd" rises above mawkishness in that it is carefully worked into the poem's decisive nullifications, its undoing of the figure of the cosmic bard and his copious songs. Envisioning himself as a drift or corpse tossed about by the ocean-mother and hugging the beach-father, Whitman not only avows his parents' continuing inescapable influence upon his psyche, but also, in a different but re-

6. See Walt Whitman, *The Early Poems and Fiction*, ed. Thomas Brasher (New York, 1963).

lated vein, his readers' inescapable and unpredictable influence upon his poetry. Although Whitman's psyche remains secure only as long as "mother" allows him a male freedom without rejecting him, his mythical persona prevails only as long as readers believe in it and intuit its songs on the songs' own terms. A historical or a poetic death can come, respectively, at the hands of a jealous, suffocating mother or of a critical reader.

Not only does Whitman reconstitute his family relations, but also, in granting the ever-present possibility of poetic death, he refashions his authorial posture, the persona he projects to readers. Though the poem begins with Whitman actively "seeking types," that is, grounding his composition process in a natural reading of nature, it ends with Whitman passively yielding himself up to readers' interpretations:

> We, capricious, brought hither, we know not whence, spread out before You,
>   up there, walking or sitting,
> Whoever you are—we too lie in drifts at your feet.
>
> (ll. 70– 71)

The "You, up there, walking or sitting" could perhaps be God or Walter Whitman, Sr.; the omnipotent but distant and neglectful attitude fits Whitman's notion of paternal authority. But Whitman's fairly conventional Christianity, his just-achieved reconciliation with his father, and the phrase "Whoever you are" (which functions more as an algebraic variable than as an appeal to a particular identity) suggest that the reader is a more likely object of the pronoun "You." No longer the amenable listener obedient to the poet's imperative bidding or the bemused onlooker fascinated by the poet's coercive physiognomy, the reader now holds the poet under *his* interpretive sway. Instead of inseminating readers with the "drift" of his "book," Whitman himself becomes a "drift" in the text who makes poetic offerings to patron critics who, he now admits, will have the final word. That is to say, knowing he has no other choice, Whitman openly submits himself to interpretation.

In terms of his genetic project, what this means is that Whitman (in this poem, at least) has abandoned his poetics, has become fully aware of its impracticality. At the foundations of his poetic ambitions was the conception of an Orphic bard whose words and tones were natural and organic and emotive enough to break with convention and tradition and penetrate readers' souls while it silenced their interpretive habits. As the middle part of "As I Ebb'd" makes clear, the medium of union (an oxymoron)—language—renders this impossible. Language does not facilitate expression, does not communicate feeling, does not realize intention in the pure and simple manner Whitman requires for his poetry to work; that is, for his songs to effect a revolution in how persons interact. Each utterance works a transformation upon the feeling it represents. Aside from the question of whether feeling is, as Whitman believes, a self-identical presence that refers to nothing but itself, this inner truth is altered, negated, reshaped by language, a differential structure whose grammar can never coincide with the grammerless "nonstructure" of feeling. In returning to his presumably ego-centered works, and noting their utter strangeness and insignificance, Whitman woefully acknowledges that the word, instead of unifying, disrupts the self and alienates it from its creations.

Whitman experiences this irreducible difference between inner feeling and outer expression as death, the death of the "Me myself" at the hands both of language (which misrepresents him) and readers (who misconstrue him). For the fact that his poetics has been undermined by linguistic difference and interpretation is not simply a matter of an idea or philosophy or literary technique being proved wrong. Because language was to be the means with which the poet was to invent himself, to forge a new identity transcending the historical contingencies and familial pressures retraining the growth of the poet's mind, the poet himself was at stake in the poetics' failure or success.

For Whitman, the self depends upon the sign. If the word remains disjoined from feeling, then the self remains "baffled" and "balked," forever poised at the threshold of fulfillment. When what does get expressed is never quite the same as what was meant or felt, each attempted disclosure becomes its opposite, an enclosure. Moving back and forth from private impulse to public utterance, Whitman experiences the shock of nonrecognition, the uncanny estrangement he feels when rereading his past recorded thoughts, leaving him to say, like Eliot's Prufrock, "That is not it at all, / That is not what I meant at all," and try to realign his words with his intention and correct the volume's "numberless deficiencies" (*Cor*, V, 272).

Though he continues to revise *Leaves of Grass* for the rest of his life, in "As I Ebb'd with the Ocean of Life" Whitman realizes the futility of ever writing the perfect poem, the unique lyric equivalent to the soul. The actual poems he views as petty fictions whose static, fragmentary, heterogeneous quality merely remind him of the ideal, transcendent self he has fallen short of becoming. Each poem marks a loss of unity, a frustration of desire, a foreboding onset of death.

Although these conclusions sound a bit too abstract and theoretical to attribute to Whitman, who, up until the war, considers theory and abstraction to be the ally of pale intellectualism and elitism, and although they may seem too speculative to apply to "As I Ebb'd with the Ocean of Life," which draws only an implicit connection between language and death, in the most famous poem added in 1860, "Out of the Cradle Endlessly Rocking," Whitman makes such an interpretation explicit.[7] Second only to "Song of Myself" in amount of critical attention received since its publication, "Out of the Cradle" brings together in one simple narrative many of the seminal themes and emotions making up the context of Whitman's poetics: love, death, sexuality, loss, and their relation to language and expression.

The scholarly tradition has interpreted "Out of the Cradle" generally as a dramatization of the poet's apprehension of death and the fundamental originary poetic inspiration it generates.[8] The boy falls from innocence into mortality and self-consciousness (the clearest symptom of which is language) and then recounts the story of his separation from

7. "Out of the Cradle" was first published by Whitman's friend Henry Clapp in the Christmas issue of the *Saturday Press*. Its first title was "A Child's Reminiscence," with the opening verse paragraph bearing the heading "Pre-Verse." In the 1860 edition, the title became "A Word Out of the Sea," with the heading "Reminiscence" placed between the first and second verse paragraphs.

8. For readings of "Out of the Cradle," see Faner, *Walt Whitman and Opera*, 86–89 and 173–77; Chase, *Walt Whitman: Reconsidered*, 120–24; Stephan Whicher, "Whitman's Awakening to Death," *Studies in Romanticism*, I (1961), 9–28; Miller, *Walt Whitman's Poetry*, 173–86; Black, *Whitman's Journeys into Chaos*, 66–76; Zweig, *Walt Whitman: The Making of the Poet*, 310–12; and Larson, *Whitman's Drama of Consensus*, 187–96. The Whicher article also appears in a collection of essays devoted partly to "Out of the Cradle": R. W. B. Lewis, ed., *The Presence of Walt Whitman* (New York, 1962). The volume contains essays by Chase, James E. Miller, Jr., and Roy Harvey Pearce. I am also indebted to Joseph Kronick's reading of "Out of the Cradle," particularly his introducing a semiotic perspective into the relation of bird-boy-poet, in *American Poetics of History*, 117–23.

nature, hoping that narration will grant him a sense of control over or at least some palliating understanding of his catastrophe. "Out of the Cradle," then, is Whitman's Romantic crisis poem, his "Tintern Abbey," "Mont Blanc," or, in its bare essentials, "Fort! Da!," the common narrative thread being the speaker's rumination upon loss or death and the compensation, not recovery, provided by poetic utterance.

The problem with this interpretation is that it presupposes a primal time of innocence, a state of mind in which the child experiences his surroundings with an unmediated vision, before cultural impositions (or Freud's *Civilization and Its Discontents*) fetter his consciousness and exile him from an unconscious participation in the world. The child "beholds God and nature face to face" (Emerson), sees the world in its "everearly candor" (Stevens), has an infallible, innate "Realometer" (Thoreau) guiding his thought. The world is transparent and the young mind is intuitive. Nature represents itself openly to hearts ready to receive it without interpreting it.

Such a scheme may be useful in studying certain aspects of Romantic nature poetry, but it does not apply to "Out of the Cradle," for in Whitman's poem nature is from the very beginning a *meaningful text* and the boy is a probing and detached exegete. The opening verse paragraph describes the boy wandering across "the sterile sands, and the fields beyond" in explicitly semiotic terms: there are "mystic play of shadows," "memories of the bird," "beginning notes of sickness and love, there in the transparent mist," "the myriad thence-aroused words," and "the word stronger and more delicious than any." Even to a child's vision, nature is a "mystic play," a melody "transparent" but "misty," an "aroused" language calling out for interpretation, beckoning the boy to reciprocate with a corresponding natural language.

Appropriately, the boy (and the reminiscing poet), "Taking all hints to use them—but swiftly leaping beyond them" (l. 21), is eager to penetrate the text, to follow the "hints" to their transcendent source. As he listens to the mockingbirds singing in the sky, instead of joining with them in their hymn of love, the "curious boy, never too close, never disturbing them," sits in the shadows "Cautiously peering, absorbing, translating" (ll. 30–31). He reads and rewrites the birds' songs, "translating" first their harmonious domestic chant and then the "he-bird's" elegiac call for his lost mate into printed, italicized English. (The bird's "words" make up almost half the poem; the poet's words function as a kind of commentary upon the conditions surrounding his "translation.") The original song, then, is not a pure self-identical, nonsemantic, Orphic outburst of feeling: the "notes" contain "meanings which I, of all men, know" (l. 60). If the song were not representational, if it did not have a memorial signified "behind" it, then the boy could not translate it. There would be no common meaning or reference to give words to; the song would have to remain in its "mocking-bird" tongue or be distorted by the boy's foreign language.

What validates the boy's translation is the fact that the bird's song is also a translation and not an original, unique eruption of feeling. As a "mocking-bird" (noted in line 2), the "solitary guest from Alabama" (l. 51) imitates "arias" already sung and arrogates for himself the instinctive cries of other birds. He is a "messenger" (l. 156). (Whitman uses this term in 1867; originally the line read "dusky demon.") Just as the boy questions him, "Is it indeed toward your mate you sing? or is it mostly to me?" (l. 145) and then recasts the songs as his own individual lament, so the "mocking-bird" borrows others' calls to express his particular sorrow. The "musical shuttles" (l. 2) from absent, unknown, original singer to forlorn, mimicking, "sad brother" (l. 9), the "mocking-bird," then to the "curious boy" "now translating the notes" (l. 69) to the aged poet, "chanter of pains and joys, uniter of here and hereafter" (l. 20), who finally renders it to the reader. Whitman places himself, the boy he was, and the bird that inspired him in a chain of interpretations without an absolute beginning or end.

In allegorizing the causes and materials beyond the poet that nevertheless shape the poetry and the impending rereadings that will reshape it, Whitman surrenders to the linguistic play that diffuses his authority and undermines his originality, the crisis he struggled so long to ward off. He frees his language from any determinate source and destination, gives up the search for a natural language of the self, and accepts "the gaiety of language" (Stevens) and "unlimited semiosis" (Peirce), even though he knows such conclusions will explode his poetics. The sign will not stay put, he now admits, which means that his Orphic dream has ended.

This is why, in "Out of the Cradle," the beginning of poetry coincides with the realization of death. At first, after hearing (and simultaneously rendering) the bird's incantatory, phrenetic "aria," the boy is swept up in a sublime sonic abandonment.

The boy extatic—with his bare feet the waves, with his hair the atmosphere
     dallying,
The love in the heart pent, now loose, now at last tumultuously bursting,
The aria's meaning, the ears, the Soul, swiftly depositing,
The strange tears down the cheeks coursing,
The colloquy there—the trio—each uttering,
The undertone—the savage old mother, incessantly crying,
To the boy's Soul's questions sullenly timing—some drowned secret hissing,
To the outsetting bard of love.

                                                    (ll. 136–43)

The "sands," the "waves," the "atmosphere," and "the notes of the wondrous bird" conspire to free the boy's "pent" "love" and to "deposit" in
his "ears" and "Soul" the meaning, "the undertone," the "drowned secret" couched in the phenomena of nature and the longings of humanity.
They form a "colloquy there . . . each uttering," enrapturing the boy's
"heart," tuning his "ears" to the Logos, and schooling his "Soul" in the
ways of oracular pronouncement.

   Assuming their organic idiom, the boy becomes the "outsetting bard
of love," his body and soul coordinated, all social constraints abolished:

For I that was a child, my tongue's use sleeping,
Now that I have heard you,
Now in a moment I know what I am for—I awake,
And already a thousand singers—a thousand songs, clearer, louder, more
     sorrowful than yours,
A thousand warbling echoes have started to life within me, never to die.

                              (ll. 146–49; Whitman later made
                                 the first two lines into one.)

Hearkening to the "he-bird's" desperate cry for his "lost mate" whose
fate lies hidden in the tantalizing yet imperturbable "sea" (the other
member of the "trio," along with the boy and the bird), the boy suddenly
finds poetic energies "starting to life within" him. With unchildlike de-
cisiveness—"I know what I am for"—he relinquishes his passive innocence, leaves behind "the peaceful child [he] was" (l. 154), and welcomes
his inevitable "destiny"—to become a spirit dedicated to poetry, singing
"the cries of unsatisfied love" (l. 153).

The poetic sounds reverberating in the boy's soul, however, are not to be confused with the *"live feeling"* Whitman eulogizes in his notebooks and prose. Whereas pure poetry erupts spontaneously from the heart, the boy's interior language derives from an external origin. Composed of "a thousand warbling *echoes*," it is an anthropomorphic translation of the mockingbird's song, which is itself an echo. Though the boy boasts that his songs are "clearer, louder, more sorrowful" than the bird's, in the next verse paragraph he promises to be faithful to his precursor, claiming that his future will be little more than a repetition of the latter's present: "O you demon, singing by yourself—projecting me, / O solitary me, listening—never more shall I cease imitating, perpetuating you" (ll. 150–51).

The newborn poet is a "project[ion]" and an "imitat[ion]," a channel-like medium "listening" to the "demon's" *"reckless, despairing carols"* (l. 104) and "perpetuating" (*perpetuus*, "to pass through") them. Though the boy, not merely a disengaged transmitter of the bird's lament, is passionately immersed in the music he renders—he sheds "strange tears" (l. 139) and feels "the fire, the sweet hell within" (l. 156)—still, that music is not entirely proper and unique to him and his wayward feelings. Notwithstanding its irregular transformation by consecutive auditors, the song precedes and succeeds each momentary "vocalization," survives beyond each individual articulation. Instead of having a local genesis and structure centered upon the "Personal Magnetism" (*NUPM*, I, 271) of the bird-boy-poet, the word is a universal, endlessly iterable "meaning," the very precondition and constitutive element of poetic identity.

"Out of the Cradle Endlessly Rocking" is not so much a dramatic poem staging the activation of Whitman's innate poetic genius as it is a "reminiscence" describing his conscious entry into reading and writing, discourse and interpretation. The boy is interpolated into a particular semiotic order, a vocal chain of signifiers bound together, in this case, by a common emotive signified, *"lonesome love"* (l. 101). Recognizing the temporal origin and destiny of his utterance, Whitman joins the procession of singer-signmakers, knowing that others will follow and "translate" his words just as he has "translated" his "brother's" "notes." The boy's singular version of the bird's lament, therefore, is less a spontaneous outburst of love springing from his awakened heart than it is a transient permutation of elegiac narrative. But it would be a mistake simply to discount the former, to say that Whitman, in introducing temporality, semiosis, and interpretation into his poetry, reduces his individual compositions to mere reiterations of conventional forms and themes.

An oversimplistic structural interpretation, by reading Whitman's poem as the discrete *parole* of a master narrative pattern or as the ideological construct of a cultural code, not only overlooks "Out of the Cradle's" peculiarity and Whitmanian-ness, its difference from other elegies, and neglects its pivotal place in the poet's canon and career. It also fails to account for what motivates the boy to adopt a hermeneutical posture toward nature in the first place. Semiotics focuses on structure, not semantics, on how a sign refers, not on what a sign means; but "Out of the Cradle Endlessly Rocking" has as its subject matter a middle ground between structure and meaning. That is to say, at the center of the poem is not a meaning or a sign but rather the tension between the two, the mercurial space and time dividing and defining them as such. More precisely, Whitman's poem is structured by (or is an outgrowth of) the conflict generated by (and generating) contrary suppositions about the nature of meaning—that is, meaning conceived of as an animating intention or feeling and meaning conceived of as an antecedent or consequent sign.

This is the fundamental opposition of "Out of the Cradle Endlessly Rocking." The boy's dilemma epitomizes the poet's: How can Whitman enunciate feelings of love and pain and longing without using an anterior form and style and without yielding his feelings up to posterior interpretations? The boy turns to the bird's song as a natural medium organically continuous with feeling, yet how does Whitman characterize his lament? First, it is a translation, a secondhand rendition of another's music. Second, it must be retranslated. After adapting the song to his own private needs, the mockingbird passes it along to the "bareheaded, barefoot" (l. 14), uncultivated child who rephrases it in human terms. (The mockingbird's fidelity to the original call and the boy's disingenuousness do not make their translations "pure," for the transformations undergone by the emotive "content" during the substitution of signifiers are not entirely due to the biases of the translators. Substitution has its own effects.) Third, and most important for the conclusion of the poem, the song is ineffective. Though the boy (and generations of readers) finds the song a poignant and beautiful articulation of a universal affliction, the song fails to achieve its specific purpose—to return the "she-bird" to her lover. It provides neither knowledge nor comfort. It neither reveals the cause of her disappearance nor does it appease the anguish debilitating the "he-bird," "the lone singer" (l. 58) who, at the end, realizes that he is "singing uselessly all the night" (l. 124).

The "aria" is "useless" not because the "he-bird" lacks any innate Orphic powers. His voice seems to possess the same qualities of "*timbre*" and "*modulation*," to reach an equal range and pathos, that "The Perfect Human Voice" (Taylor, the opera singer Bettini, Hicks, and so on) does. Like the sometimes bardic, sometimes furtive, but always affecting voice in "Song of Myself," the "he-bird" moves from direct, commanding entreaty—"*High and clear I shoot my voice over the waves, / Surely you must know who is here, / You must know who I am my love*" (ll. 83–85)—to quieter, hypnotic, humlike tones—"*Soft! Let me just murmur, . . . With this just-sustained note I announce myself to you, / This gentle call is for you my love*" (ll. 106, 113–14). It is the song that fails, not the singer. It is the language itself that prevents the bird from recuperating the obscure lost object of desire. As a derivative utterance, the bird's song makes present only the anterior language it represents. The lost object and the feelings bound up with it exist beyond the order of signs and hence remain dark and unreachable.

Singing brings about more songs, not an end of singing, which a recuperation would accomplish. Though the "two guests from Alabama" (l. 26) sang to each other before the catastrophe, the last line in their duet ("*If we two but keep together*," l. 40) indicates that their inspiration is not so much their happiness in being together as it is their fear of imminent separation. Having resorted to words for satisfaction, for a restoration of domestic unity, the "he-bird" condemns himself to an endless retelling of his tragedy: "*Murmur! Murmur on! / O murmurs—you yourselves make me continue to sing, I know not why*" (lines later deleted; they originally followed line 124 after a space). Now it is the "murmuring," not the underlying feelings, that incites him to sing. Once articulation has taken the place of pure, undifferentiated feeling, one can never return to the simplicity of primitive, instinctual action and perception. The thing itself remains mediated and desire is eternalized. Intended for solace, the bird's song turns into a never-ending, self-defeating strategy bringing no physical or "metaphysical comfort."

Of course, the idea of a preinterpretive innocence or a prelapserian childhood golden age is a myth, a fictional memory constructed from the nostalgic perspective of self-conscious language users. As we have seen, even in "Out of the Cradle Endlessly Rocking" mediation and semiosis are effectively at work in the boy, the birds, and nature from the very beginning. Nature unveils to the boy the semiotic nature of life, the fact that he lives in a world of interpretations and translations, a world in which meaning and truth and feeling and reality lie hidden or, more precisely, are a fugitive function of their ever-present yet insubstantial representatives. The boy must decide whether to become a willing participant in "unlimited semiosis" or to struggle futilely against it, to accept the temporal, revisionary character of his utterance or to try to stabilize and consecrate it, to forestall interpretation and halt the semiotic mutations his poems will suffer.

As we have seen, most of the time Whitman's poetics embrace the latter hope. Whitman's poet-figure manifests the authority and allure and veracity necessary to arrest interpretation—"The presence of the great poet conquers—not parleying, or struggling or prepared attempts" (*PW*, II, 438)—or at least to confine semiosis to a straight and true passage of feeling from one soul to another. Ideally, *Leaves of Grass* acts as a spirited transparent medium organically grounded in the inarticulate speech of the heart. Because it already accords with feeling, it need not be comprehended. In this way, feeling-presence is preserved, and Whitman's unique experience stays permanently fixed as the central force guiding readers' understanding.

"Out of the Cradle Endlessly Rocking" subverts this conception of poetry and poets. The communicative model Whitman sets up in the poem belies the notion of original, heart-centered poetry insusceptible to interpretation. Exchanges of feeling rely upon an undeniably semiotic process that prevents any individual from mastering the writerly-readerly effects such exchanges are subject to. It may be objected that the poem's conclusion does, in fact, postulate an end to or a controlling center of discourse, of composition and interpretation, but actually the opposite is the case. Presumably, what overrides or circumscribes signification would be a nonsign, a "transcendental signified" that, although governing the play of signifiers, would remain apart from and unaffected by the game it regulates. But at the end of the poem, the boy asks for and receives "some clew" (l. 158), a "vapor, a look, a song," not a thing in itself, a loving comrade, a mystical truth, or anything else that would answer his longing and end his song of desire and loss:

A word then, (for I will conquer it,)
The word final, superior to all,
Subtle, sent up—what is it?—I listen;
Are you whispering it, and have been all the time, you sea-waves?
Is that it from your liquid rims and wet sands?

(ll. 160–64)

Though "final, superior to all," "the key, the word up from the waves" (l. 179) is still a word, a message that must be "whispered" and "listened" to. In asking for a sign and not a presence, the boy resists the vanity and fruitlessness of trying to penetrate the essence of nature and instead acknowledges the inevitable prevalence of mediation. And the "sea-waves," instead of unveiling a "transcendental signified" that would organize and delimit the anxiety-causing play of semiosis—"O I fear it is henceforth chaos!" (this phrase was later deleted)—and disclose to the boy his "destination," can proffer only an empty signifier, an enigmatic name devoid of any fixed meaning or reference:

Answering, the sea,
Delaying not, hurrying not,
Whispered me through the night, and very plainly before daybreak,
Lisped to me constantly the low and delicious word DEATH,
And again Death—ever Death, Death, Death,
Hissing melodious, neither like the bird, nor like my aroused child's heart,
But edging near, as privately for me, rustling at my feet,
And creeping thence steadily up to my ears,
Death, Death, Death, Death, Death.

(ll. 165–73)

What critical language can adequately explain these lines, which address themselves to (if not transgress) the boundaries of sense and draw an occult connection between language and death? To interpret the sea's blank, peremptory iteration of "the low and delicious word death" solely as the boy's awakening to mortality and to the ever-impending loss of love and security is to ignore the poem's sustained and profound problematizing of meaning and expression. "Whispering" and "lisping" its repetitive language of annihilation, "hissing melodious" a "rustling,"

150

"creeping" monotone signifying nothing, the "sea" uncovers the semiotic impasse created by the boy's having subjected feelings to a signifying order. By disrupting the unmediated plenitude of auto-affection and introducing the exterior sign into the soul, or, more accurately, by realizing the sign's paradoxical interiority in all human experiences from the very beginning (the "beginning" being a fictional afterthought), the boy admits a gap into intuition and expression and suspends indefinitely the reappropriation of purified feeling.

Death is the name for this marginal void. Death can only be understood as the absence of its original, life, as body without spirit, form without content, sign without intention. "Death" is the signifier par excellence, the sign signifying signification itself. It is neither a thing nor an event, but rather a term loaded with insignificance, a name for that noncause that makes meaning and expression possible.

"Death, Death, Death, Death, Death"—the forever *pen*ultimate iteration, the unbridled repetition determining and de-terminating Whitman's poetry. It is the "fitful risings and fallings' (l. 9), the "echoes" and "reverberations" (ll. 149 and 152) randomly measuring out his verse and prolonging it, opening it to citation and mimicry, forestalling any final settlement upon a meaning, an intention, a feeling, a truth. Iteration determines the term, disseminates its content across a structural field, diffuses it into a past and a future that has no termination.

Lest this movement be confused with the antipoetic or the antihuman, we must remember that iteration (or "death") *is* poetry. Not simply an absolute interruption but more graphically a pulsating, rhythmic, signifying indication of thinking and feeling and speaking, "death" is indeed the corporate *life* of poetry. After hearing the sea whisper its sonorous, mystical, "low and delicious" litany, Whitman recalls, "My own songs, awaked from that hour, / And with them the key, the word up from the waves, / The word of the sweetest song, and all songs" (ll. 178–80). "Death" marks "the beginning of [his] great career," the substance of which is "the thousand responsive songs [sung] at random" (l. 177), without any determinate, meaning-full origin or destination. Though a beginning, however, "death" is not a fixed identity or presence. It is an evanescent boundary, a liminal dividing line between now and then, or, in the context of the poem, between text and pre-text. Hence, "Death" is also an end, a posterior boundary reified when *Leaves of Grass* is yielded up to the negating action of interpretation, when Whitman's songs take their turn as pre-texts for subsequent poems or, even worse, criticism. In other words, what Whitman realizes at the conclusion of "Out of the Cradle Endlessly Rocking" is his liability to the mortal effects of the sign, to the derivational quality of all utterance, and to the displacing, sequential pattern of interpretation.

Natural writing and natural reading are the necessary but inapplicable constituents of Whitman's logocentric poetics, a theory undertaking to fend off the deviant operations of the arbitrary sign. Actual writing and actual reading, succumbing as they do to desire and convention and history and semiosis, decenter the Orphic poet and undermine the central thrust of the poetics—to create and preserve a closed circuit of feeling transmission. Language and death allow difference and mediation, indeterminacy and misconstruction, to infiltrate communication. The sign may no longer be regarded as a simple transition, a momentary formulation that carries out its transportational duty and dissolves without leaving a trace. And poetry may no longer be considered a transparent medium embodying but not supplementing a more vital, natural medium—feeling.

Accordingly, Whitman abandons his early poetics. Although the later prose pieces maintain an interest in oratory, slang, physiognomy, "magnetism," and other linguistic and semiotic media with which Whitman concerned himself in the 1850s (for example, "Slang in America" dates from 1885, "Father Taylor (and Oratory)" from 1887), poems appearing in editions following the Civil War seem to emerge from a more static and controlled aesthetic. Specifically, one finds that Whitman more and more often opts for a style and a subject matter in which the "I" in linguistic process—reading and writing, translating and interpreting—has all but vanished.

For instance, of the sixty-five poems in the late collection, *Sands at Seventy,* only twenty-one contain the pronoun "I." Of those, only six go beyond making a single passing reference. Instead of dramatizing the poet as a thoroughly engaged interpreter of nature's textual wonders, an inquisitive writer implicated in the semiotic processes he would seek to master or ignore, these and other late poems acquaint the reader with a watchful but anonymous and somewhat uninvolved observer carefully recording his impressions of life. The problematics of observation and recording are suppressed, and the poems are scaled down into brief reports of an image or feeling or insight the poet immediately intuits.

Compared with the precarious, multi-leveled journeys of interpretation Whitman embarks upon in "Song of Myself," "Crossing Brooklyn Ferry," "Out of the Cradle Endlessly Rocking," and so on, the bard's later descriptions and narratives are so vague and detached that they make the "I" almost too universal and general to be recognizable as "plain old Walt."

I offer this admittedly oversimplified characterization of Whitman's later practice (there are some exceptions, but the general trend is clear) neither as an evaluative judgment nor in order to demand of him, like D. H. Lawrence does, "What have you done with yourself? With your own individual self? For it sounds as if it had all leaked out of you, leaked into the universe?"[9] Rather, I mean to assert that Whitman's "language experiment" ended in 1860, that he recognized the impracticality of his poetic project and adopted a different attitude toward his role as a poet and toward the nature of poetic language. That recognition comes when he is faced with the fatal consequences of semiosis. To escape the transitory nature of individual utterance in a semiotic universe, Whitman, in later poems, removes the poet from the field of textual play. As noted above, instead of being an active, translating seer and sayer operating within the poem, Whitman tries to withdraw to the framing perspective of aesthetic distance, a secure refuge immune to the textual machinations occurring in the world around him.

Likewise, his attempts to safeguard his language against semiosis, to forestall future interpretations and transfigurations, signal his mortality and place him among the dead poets whose works "transcendent and new" (*PW*, II, 437) poetry must leave behind. But, whereas Whitman in the 1850s sought to discourage criticism and "translation" by proclaiming the organicism of his language, in later years he does so by his increasing usage of an ever more abstract and nonfigural diction and imagery.

To confirm Whitman's movement toward abstraction, one need only compare his description of the self in Section 8 of the well-known "Passage to India" (1871) with almost any prewar description of the self, for example, with that of Section 4 of "Song of Myself." Whereas in the latter poem, the "Me myself" is a concrete, pictorial delineation of a physique "Looking with sidecurved head" at "the game" of society

9. D. H. Lawrence, *Studies in Classic American Literature* (New York, 1961), 165.

(ll. 78–79), the "actual Me" of the former poem is a depersonalized, bodiless "soul" out to master the universe:

> Swiftly I shrivel at the thought of God,
> At Nature and its wonders, Time and Space and Death,
> But that I, turning, call to thee, O soul, thou actual Me,
> And lo! thou gently masterest the orbs,
> Thou matest Time, smilest content at Death,
> And fillest, swellest full, the vastnesses of Space.
>
> (ll. 206–11)

The vacuous, featureless images here represent Whitman's "soul" rescuing him from intimidation and submissiveness at the "sight" of sublimity, when the universe's cosmic elements approach him directly and expose his utter paltriness. Like a "god," the "soul" plainly encounters "Time" and "Death," triumphing over both instantly, and then impregnates "Space" with its own teeming, prolific "love" (l. 214).

Through this appeal to the transcendent part of his being, which easily and "gently masterest the orbs," sexlessly "matest Time," complacently "smilest content at Death," and immaculately inseminates "the vastnesses of Space," Whitman quickly but unconvincingly turns his anxiety to omnipotence. The "actual Me's" surety and ease and smooth confidence render its claims trivial. The ethereal sexuality signifies a retreat from, not an expansion of, Whitman's erotic desires. The abruptness with which the "soul" transforms the universe erases the tension and guilt the poet felt earlier when he hesitated to "re-write" nature, when he wanted to inscribe a natural poem yet feared that doing so would supervene a layer of factitious, conventional notations upon the natural order of things.

Not only has the action incredibly neutralized the poet's interpretive dilemma and dissolved the self in abstraction, but also, on a stylistic level, the poem's diction and syntax have lost connection with the concrete. Instead of, say, allegorizing "Time and Space and Death" and making them figural representatives of metaphysical concepts, Whitman merely capitalizes their arbitrary names and treats them as sufficiently corporeal. Instead of using the familiar "you" as he would to lovers and friends and comrades, Whitman addresses his "soul" with the formal "Thou." And instead of using the common verb ending, Whitman selects the archaic "-est" in order to lend gravity to the scene. All three usages, as well as the inversions and the convoluted syntax, Whitman previously would have regarded as artificial poeticisms alien to democratic society, false elevations of discourse in the service of elitism and tradition. Judged by the standards of his early poetics, "Passage to India" would not qualify as poetry, for its language (and most of the language of the later editions) corresponds neither to real things nor to real passions as he understands them.

While Whitman's poetry was becoming more and more abstract and prosaic, Whitman the man was becoming more and more "phenomenal" and poetic. It has been amply documented by Allen, Kaplan, Zweig, and other biographers that from the war onward, Whitman shapes his life and character around the mythical persona of "the good gray poet," the Romantic figure of the kindly native bard created by O'Connor's polemical pamphlet.[10] In countless newspaper pieces, letters, conversations, and in late poems, Whitman concocts a misleading facade that, although it may perhaps satisfy a fantasy or repress self-doubts, certainly comes at the expense of his actual experiences and memories (his "real Me"?). Using a rhetoric that poses as natural and spontaneous but is, in truth, entirely calculated, Whitman spends most of his time surreptitiously aggrandizing himself and attacking those "enemies" who regard him as anything less than America's literary patriarch. He insists that biographers (notably Bucke) send him their manuscripts so he can "authenticate" them (always sacrificing verity for wish-fulfillment); he revises poems; he sends "memoranda," "diary notes," and "travel reports" concerning his "latest" to magazines and journals, all in an effort to foster a fictitious self-image. Not only his early poems but also his early prose, letters, and documents, Whitman either destroys or scrupulously fits to his fabricated identity in the last decade of his life to the extent that, as Kaplan says, "By the time he died scarcely a period in his life had not been 'revised' in one way or another."[11]

And yet his attempts to subsume his life and his self into a poetic fiction became such an obsession that they supplanted the historical "Per-

10. Reprinted in Bucke, *Walt Whitman*, 99–130.
11. Kaplan, *Walt Whitman: A Life*, 19.

sonality" Whitman claimed was to occupy the center of his poetry. Although he longed to signify feeling in a transparent medium that would preserve the ego's primacy and integrity, the opposite occurred. Instead of Whitman's structuring his poetry along the lines of his free, tameless moods and impressions, the poetry has structured a bardic identity (a "literatus") along the lines of its figurative conventions. He becomes a trope, a literary persona with its own tradition and expectations. This is another reason why Whitman, in "As I Ebb'd with the Ocean of Life," singles out his poems as his own worst enemy and why, in "Out of the Cradle Endlessly Rocking," he associates language and singing with death. At first, an open, indigenous, organic poetic idiom seemed to provide an adequately expressive means of publicizing feeling, but, as it turns out, publication spells the death of feeling.

Language, especially writing, divides feeling, turns it away from itself, versifies the self beyond recognition. Speech or gesture may, if we were to grant relative degrees of conventionality or arbitrariness, produce less anxiety (over interpretation) and less self-estrangement and forebodings of mortality (when one reflects upon one's no longer recognizable creations) than writing does. But still, in poetry, aural and pictographic signs and the feelings they embody can only be represented through the letter. Whitman entreats us to ignore that fact—"The words of my book nothing, the drift of it everything" ("Shut Not Your Doors")—but nevertheless, the printed word and all its effects relentlessly interpose themselves between poet and readers and between Whitman and himself.

The assumption of a rhetorical mask completes Whitman's abandonment of his poetics and his capitulation to language and writing. Surely other motives drove him to suppress his "Me myself" (for example, a fatherly identity probably made his relations with younger men less threatening), but the literary basis of his newfound role indicates that his experiences with poetry and poetics and criticism from 1855 to 1860 had a shaping influence over the course of his later life. The question Whitman posed during those years (and more forcefully than any other writer of his time) was whether the sign could be naturalized, whether he could institute a native vernacular poetic discourse that remained faithful to pure human being. As he discovered, not only was the sign utterly conventional but the original feelings that the sign should and *must* express became implicated in their representative's semiotic variance. How else, then, could he end his "language experiment" than to don an identity that is thoroughly conventional and superficial and then to use expertly all the rhetorical, fraudulent, and manipulative strategies that language, in all its arbitrariness and dissimulation, places at his disposal, the signifying play that gives his persona a false depth, like a face in a mirror or a picture on a frontispiece?

Postscript

In writing a poetry that belied its transcendental purpose, in taking a linguistic turn and abandoning himself to the eddies of interpretation, Whitman concluded his language experiment and went on with his life. He continued to write poems, but those exercises were most often not experimental, but merely exemplary. That is, they simply put into practice an Orphic principle, all the while neglecting or suppressing the inconsistencies and contradictions of that unprincipled principle and minimizing the quandaries of that promiscuous, impractical practice.

For the most part, later poems neither explore the historical and linguistic circumstances of their coming into being nor do they anticipate their destiny, the historical and linguistic transformations they will undergo. The anxiety has disappeared, and it seems that, after 1860, Whitman is secure in writing a poetry blissfully ignorant of the problematics of representation and interpretation that haunted his early work. But his security does not change the fact that much of his later writing involves obsessive self-revision of and reflection upon his "unmediated" language, and hence leaves its own mark or diacritical scar upon its "face."

Having relinquished his poetics of presence-feeling, Whitman no longer regards representation and interpretation as problems, as mutations threatening to disfigure some treasured natural origin. Contrary to the poet's expectations, the undoing of his early ambitions does not aggravate the Whitmanian dilemma—how to keep transmission from thwarting its intention—but rather, that collapse resolves it. Whitman's "failure" does not, as one might assume, condemn him to subjugation by linguistic structures whose prison house sterilizes desire and paralyzes the will, annuls morality, and hinders commitment and action.

Though the "realities" now appear to be thoroughly textualized (the reverse of Whitman's initial goal), this in no way means that the poet can no longer dwell poetically and humanistically, or that his remodeled poetic dwelling has no room for the sociopolitical phase of Whitman's undertaking. If anything, the opposite is the case, for what liberal reforms or "perfectibilities" in society are possible, what open debates can take place, within a poetics that casts all reforms as predetermined return to nature and all proper discourse as a single-minded reinstatement of organicism?

By 1860, in the poetry if not in the prose, Whitman perhaps realizes that the liberation he craved, the freedom of expression held out to New World inhabitants by America's progressive constitutional laws, lay not in an original Orphic language spontaneously generating from feeling but in a language freed from the constraints of origin altogether. It may be that originality, not convention, is the stifling limitation slowing the progress of democracy.

To Whitman, an origin now appears, when stripped of its theological privilege, as regulatory, retrospective, and conservative. And a language affirming an origin (language as Logos) becomes dogmatic, univocal, authoritative. In America, a nation whose revolutionary beginning occurred through a negation of origin and whose manifest destiny was ceaseless expansion, it also becomes antidemocratic. (While "Facing West from California's Shores," Whitman writes, he and, by implication, America are still "Inquiring, tireless, seeking what is yet unfound.") Ever sliding into an "official story" authenticated by correspondence to institutionalized "truths," not by individual experience, a discourse shadowed by its putative origin suits authority's need to control individuals and information much better than a discourse that questions origins, that treats even its own espoused ideas critically. To force, legislate, or shame individuals into a manageable "en masse," authority centers its rhetoric upon some foundational principle—for example, nature, racial purity, the divine example of a religious figure, or (in the case of the Reagan administration) "freedom." That principle must itself remain uninterrogated, for a modern authority's greatest fear is that close examination of its sanctioned foundations might reveal its rhetoric's utter incoherence or fraudulence. Analysis would expose the strategies of inclusion and exclusion that support vested interests by disguising themselves as the natural state of things.

Whitman's writings play out this dispute, the postulation of an origin and the exposure or recognition of that postulation as untenable. Whitman proposes a poetics of feeling, a poetics in which "the mere words . . . disappear," in which theory, composition, reading, and revision have no consequential role. He then proceeds to write a poetry about writing and reading, a poetry explicitly calling attention to its textual nature. With *Leaves of Grass* contravening its stated goals, Whitman winds up criticizing his own ambitions, a gesture implicitly signaling the poet's awareness of the liabilities of presence.

The first three editions, culminating in the *Sea-Drift* lyrics, chronicle this adjustment, this rite of passage wherein the poet gives up his last nostalgias, emancipates himself from the specter of a lost plenitude, and accepts being a wayward drift in the unpredictable republic of letters. Once Whitman has admitted the historical and linguistic contingencies of his utterance, once he has recognized that there is no unconditional surrender of feeling to language, the theoretical problematic informing Whitman's early works dissipates and the need to write poetry ends.

With the experiment finalized, no more investigation is necessary or even worthwhile, for any further attempt to insert a natural idiom into American literary discourse would give way to the project's inevitable outcome—the sovereignty of language and the displacement of nature. Fending off this result was the purpose of writing poems, but with the nostalgic, naïve, Rousseauistic thrust of Whitman's poetics removed from practical consideration, there is no conflict for the poems to explore. To be sure, there are other important conflicts in *Leaves of Grass* than expressive, compositional, and interpretive clashes—namely, political, sexual, and religious ones—but take away the linguistic dilemmas framing those thematic conflicts and Whitman's poetry becomes notoriously dull.

Leaves of Grass began not with an inspiration, but with a menace to inspiration. Whitman's poems came to life when a break occurred in the line of communication, when loss or distance or transformation threatened to expose feeling exchanges to misrepresentation and decay. The deciding issue was whether poetry could traverse that distance and maintain its origin's purity, whether any language could facilitate a receiving experience identical to the originating experience.

As long as Whitman believed, despite mounting evidence to the contrary, in the possibility of repetition without a difference, he found he had a fertile crisis to work with, an enabling antagonism whose field of action was the poem. When that contest culminated in the ascendance of the linguistic field itself, Whitman acknowledged that the governing law of communication, of all human relations, was perpetual traversal, not origin and destination in a closed circuit of souls. Succumbing to the postmodern condition, Whitman, intentionally or not, reduced his ideal communion to language games, specifically to the contracts poets make and break with precursors and disciples and themselves. Instead of orchestrating what he thought was fragmented society into a harmonized democratic community, Whitman's poetry served only to distinguish the network of signs and relations that constituted society as such.

Bibliography

Works by Whitman

An American Primer. Edited by Horace Traubel. Cambridge, Mass., 1904.
The Correspondence of Walt Whitman. Edited by Edwin Haviland Miller. 6 vols. New York, 1961–77.
Daybooks and Notebooks. Edited by William White. 3 vols. New York, 1978.
The Early Poems and the Fiction. Edited by Thomas Brasher. New York, 1963.
The Eighteenth Presidency. Edited by Edward F. Grier. Lawrence, Kans., 1956.
Leaves of Grass: Comprehensive Reader's Edition. Edited by Harold W. Blodgett and Sculley Bradley. New York, 1965.
Leaves of Grass: A Textual Variorum of the Printed Poems. Edited by Sculley Bradley, Harold W. Blodgett, Arthur Golden, and William White. 3 vols. New York, 1980.
New York Dissected: A Sheaf of Recently Discovered Newspaper Articles by the Author of "Leaves of Grass." Edited by Emory Holloway and Ralph Adimari. New York, 1936.
Notebooks and Unpublished Prose Manuscripts. Edited by Edward F. Grier. 6 vols. New York, 1984.
Prose Works, 1892. Edited by Floyd Stovall. 2 vols. New York, 1963–64.
Walt Whitman's Autograph Revisions of the Analysis of "Leaves of Grass" (For Dr. R. M. Bucke's "Walt Whitman"). Introductory essay by Quentin Anderson; text notes by Stephan Railton. New York, 1974.

Works About Whitman

Allen, Gay Wilson. *The Solitary Singer: A Critical Biography of Walt Whitman.* Chicago, 1955.

Anderson, Quentin. *The Imperial Self: An Essay in American Literary and Cultural History.* New York, 1971.

Aspiz, Harold. *Walt Whitman and the Body Beautiful.* Urbana, 1980.

Asselineau, Roger. *The Evolution of Walt Whitman.* Translated by Richard P. Adams and Roger Asselineau. 2 vols. Cambridge, Mass., 1960–62.

Bedient, Calvin. "Orality and Power (Whitman's 'Song of Myself')." *Delta: Revue de Centre d'Études et de Recherche sur les Écrivains du Sud aux États-Unis,* XVI (1983), 79–94.

———. "Walt Whitman: Overruled." *Salmagundi,* LVIII–LIX (1982–83), 326–46.

Black, Stephan. *Whitman's Journeys into Chaos: A Psychoanalytic Study of the Creative Process.* Princeton, 1975.

Bloom, Harold. *Agon: Towards a Theory of Revisionism.* New York, 1982.

———. *A Map of Misreading.* New York, 1975.

———. *Poetry and Repression: Revisionism from Blake to Stevens.* New Haven, 1976.

Bove, Paul. *Destructive Poetics: Heidegger and Modern American Poetry.* New York, 1980.

Breitweiser, Mitchell Robert. "Who Speaks in Whitman's Poems?" *Bucknell Review,* XXVIII (1983), 121–43.

Bucke, Richard Maurice. *Cosmic Consciousness.* New York, 1923.

———. *Walt Whitman.* Philadelphia, 1883.

Burroughs, John. *Whitman: A Study.* Boston, 1896.

Bychowski, Gustav. "Walt Whitman: A Study in Sublimation." *Psychoanalysis and the Social Sciences,* III (1951), 223–61.

Cady, Joseph. "Not Happy in the Capitol: Homosexuality and the *Calamus* Poems." In *Walt Whitman: Here and Now,* edited by Joann Krieg. Westport, Conn., 1985.

Cavitch, David. *My Soul and I: The Inner Life of Walt Whitman.* Boston, 1985.

Chari, V. K. *Whitman in the Light of Vedantic Mysticism.* Lincoln, Nebr., 1964.

Chase, Richard. *Walt Whitman Reconsidered.* New York, 1955.

Durand, Regis. "The Anxiety of Performance." *New Literary History,* XII (1980), 167–76.

Erkkila, Betsy. *Whitman the Political Poet.* New York, 1988.

Faner, Robert D. *Walt Whitman and Opera.* Philadelphia, 1951.

Feidelson, Charles. *Symbolism and American Literature.* Chicago, 1953.

Finkel, William L. "Sources of Walt Whitman's Manuscript Notes on Physique." *American Literature,* XXII (1950), 29–53.

———. "Walt Whitman's Manuscript Notes on Oratory." *American Literature,* XXII (1950), 308–31.

Hindus, Milton, ed. *Walt Whitman: The Critical Heritage.* London, 1971.

Hollis, C. Carroll. *Language and Style in "Leaves of Grass."* Baton Rouge, 1983.

———. "Recasting *Leaves of Grass:* Whitman's Moral Vocabulary in the Early and Late Poems." In *The Cast of Consciousness: Concepts of Mind in British and American Romanticism,* edited by Beverly Taylor and Robert Bain. New York, 1987.

———. "Whitman and William Swinton: A Cooperative Friendship." *American Literature,* XXX (1959), 425–49.

Holloway, Emory. *Whitman: An Interpretation in Narrative.* New York, 1926.

———. "Whitman's Embryonic Verse." *Southwest Review,* X (1925), 28–40.

Irwin, John. *American Hieroglyphics: The Symbol of the Egyptian Hieroglyphic in the American Renaissance.* New Haven, 1980.

James, William. *The Varieties of Religious Experience.* Cambridge, Mass., 1985.

Kaplan, Justin. *Walt Whitman: A Life.* New York, 1980.

Kennedy, William Sloane. *Reminiscences of Walt Whitman.* London, 1896.

Killingsworth, M. Jimmie. "Sentimentality and Homosexuality in Whitman's *Calamus* Poems." *ESQ: A Journal of the American Renaissance,* XXIX (1983), 144–53.

———. *Whitman's Poetry of the Body: Sexuality, Politics, and the Text.* Chapel Hill, N.C., 1989.

Kronick, Joseph G. *American Poetics of History: From Emerson to the Moderns.* Baton Rouge, 1984.

Larson, Kerry C. *Whitman's Drama of Consensus.* Chicago, 1988.

Lawrence, D. H. *Studies in Classic American Literature.* New York, 1961.

Lewis, R. W. B. *The American Adam: Innocence, Tragedy, and Tradition in the Nineteenth Century.* Chicago, 1955.

———, ed. *The Presence of Walt Whitman.* New York, 1962.

Loving, Jerome. *Emerson, Whitman, and the American Muse.* Chapel Hill, N.C., 1982.

Martin, Robert K. *The Homosexual Tradition in American Poetry.* Austin, Tex., 1979.

———. " 'Song of Myself': Homosexual Dream and Vision." *Partisan Review,* XLII (1975), 80–96.

Matthiessen, F. O. *American Renaissance: Art and Expression in the Age of Emerson and Whitman.* New York, 1941.

Miller, Edwin Haviland. *Walt Whitman's Poetry: A Psychological Journey.* New York, 1968.

Miller, James E., Jr. *A Critical Guide to "Leaves of Grass."* Chicago, 1957.

Pearce, Roy Harvey. *The Continuity of American Poetry.* Princeton, 1961.

Pease, Donald. *Visionary Compacts: American Renaissance Writings in Cultural Contexts.* Madison, Wis., 1987.

Poirier, Richard. *A World Elsewhere: The Place of Style in American Literature.* New York, 1966.

Pound, Ezra. "What I Feel About Walt Whitman." Edited by Herbert Bergman and reprinted in *American Literature,* XXVII (1955), 56–61.

Reiss, Edmund. "Whitman's Debt to Animal Magnetism." *PMLA,* LXXVIII (1963), 80–88.

Sedgwick, Eve. *Between Men: English Literature and Male Homosocial Desire.* New York, 1985.

Stovall, Floyd. *The Foreground of "Leaves of Grass."* Charlottesville, Va., 1974.

Strauch, Carl. "The Structure of Walt Whitman's 'Song of Myself.'" *English Journal,* XXVII (1938), 597–607.

Swinton, William. *Rambles Among Words.* New York, 1864.

Thomas, M. Wynn. *The Lunar Light of Whitman's Poetry.* Cambridge, Mass., 1987.

Traubel, Horace, et al., eds. *With Walt Whitman in Camden.* Vol. I, Boston, 1906. Vol. II, New York, 1908. Vol. III, New York, 1914. Vol. IV, edited by Sculley Bradley, Philadelphia, 1953. Vol. V, edited by Gertrude Traubel, Carbondale, Ill., 1964. Vol. VI, edited by Gertrude Traubel and William White, Carbondale, Ill., 1982.

Traubel, Horace, Richard Maurice Bucke, and Thomas B. Harned, eds. *In Re Walt Whitman.* Philadelphia, 1893.

Trowbridge, John T. *My Own Story, with Recollections of Noted Persons.* Boston, 1904.

Warren, James Perrin. "Dating Whitman's Language Studies." *Walt Whitman Quarterly Review,* I (1983), 1–7.

———. "Whitman as Ghostwriter: The Case of *Rambles Among Words.*" *Walt Whitman Quarterly Review,* II (1984), 23–30.

Whicher, Stephan. "Whitman's Awakening to Death." *Studies in Romanticism,* I (1961), 9–28.

Zweig, Paul. *Walt Whitman: The Making of the Poet.* New York, 1985.

Other Works Consulted

Austin, John L. *How to Do Things with Words.* Edited by J. O. Urmson and Marina Sbisa. Cambridge, Mass., 1962.

Burke, Kenneth. "I, Eye, Aye—Emerson's Early Essay 'Nature': Thoughts on the Machinery of Transcendence." In *Transcendentalism and Its Legacy*, edited by Myron Simon and Thornton H. Parsons. Ann Arbor, 1966.

de Man, Paul. *Allegories of Reading: Figural Language in Rousseau, Nietzsche, Rilke, and Proust.* New Haven, 1979.

——. *The Resistance to Theory.* Minneapolis, 1986.

——. "Sign and Symbol in Hegel's *Aesthetics.*" *Critical Inquiry*, VIII (1982), 761–77.

Derrida, Jacques. *Of Grammatology.* Translated by Gayatri Chakravorty Spivak. Baltimore, 1974.

——. *Writing and Difference.* Translated by Alan Bass. Chicago, 1978.

de Saussure, Ferdinand. *Course in General Linguistics.* Edited by Charles Bally, Albert Sechehaye, and Albert Reidlinger. Translated by Wade Baskin. New York, 1959.

de Tocqueville, Alexis. *Democracy in America.* Edited by J. P. Mayer. Translated by George Lawrence. Garden City, N.Y., 1969.

Emerson, Edward Waldo, ed. *The Complete Works of Ralph Waldo Emerson.* 12 vols. Boston and New York, 1903–1904.

Freud, Sigmund. *Standard Edition of the Complete Psychological Works.* Edited and translated by James Strachey *et al.* 24 vols. London, 1953–74.

Hegel, Georg Wilhelm Friedrich. *The Phenomenology of Mind.* Edited and translated by J. B. Baillie. New York, 1931.

Heidegger, Martin. *An Introduction to Metaphysics.* Translated by Ralph Manheim. New Haven, 1959.

Kant, Immanuel. *Critique of Judgment.* Translated by J. H. Bernard. New York, 1951.

Lacan, Jacques. *Ecrits: A Selection.* Translated by Alan Sheridan. New York, 1977.

Melville, Herman. *Moby-Dick; or The Whale.* Edited by Harrison Hayford and Hershel Parker. New York, 1967.

Miller, J. Hillis. "The Triumph of Theory, the Resistance to Reading, and the Question of the Material Base." *PMLA*, CII (1987), 281–92.

Nairne, Charles Murray. *Oration Delivered by Charles Murray Nairne, M.A., Before the Philoclean & Peithessophian Societies of Rutgers College, New Burnswick, N.J.* New York, 1857.

Peirce, Charles Sanders. *The Collected Papers of Charles Sanders Peirce.* 8 vols. Vols. I–VI edited by Charles Hartshorne and Paul Weiss. Vols. VII–VIII edited by Arthur W. Burks. Cambridge, Mass., 1931–58.

Riddel, Joseph N. "Coup de Man; or, The Uses and Abuses of Semiotics." *Cultural Critique*, IV (1986), 81–109.

Sheridan, Thomas. *Lectures on the Art of Reading.* 2 vols. London, 1775.

Stevens, Wallace. *Collected Poems.* New York, 1954.

Webster, Noah. *An American Dictionary of the English Language.* New York, 1828.

Williams, William Carlos. *Imaginations.* Edited by Webster Schott. New York, 1971.

Index